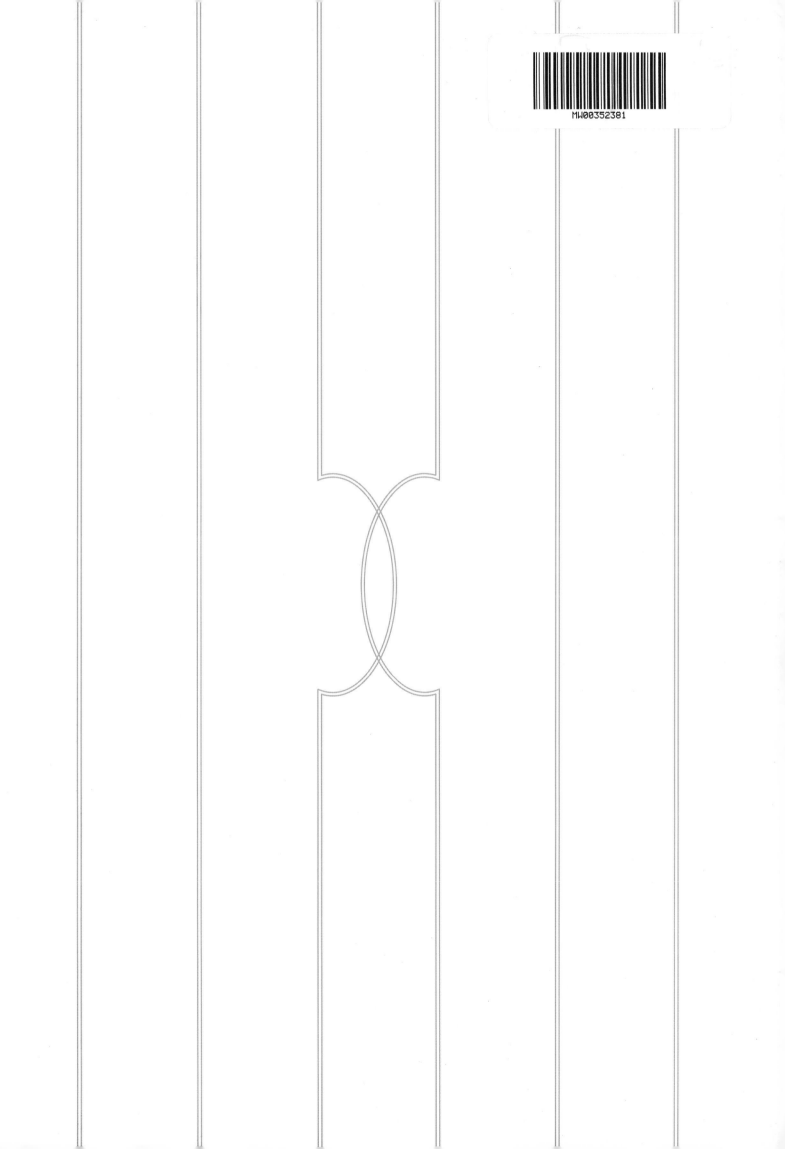

"It's totally obvious to me that Geoffrey Bradfield designs environments in layers, making a syntax where a sculpture or a painting will be the object or the focal point of the whole enterprise. This can only come from a person with a deep devotion, respect, and love for art. You get that when you look at his work."

—JULIAN SCHNABEL

© Geoffrey Bradfield 2012

Printed in China

ISBN: 978-0-917841-03-3

First printing 2012
1 2 3 4 5 6 7 8 9 10

Distributed by ACC Distribution
6 West 18th Street
Suite 4 B
NYC, NY 10011
phone: 1-800-252-5231
e mail: info@antiquecc.com
www.accdistribution.com

PHOTOGRAPHY CREDITS

Sean Finnigan: Front Jacket, 1-2, 5, 9, 17, 19, 20-21, 30-31, 32, 33,
34, 36-37, 38, 39, 43, 46-47, 50, 57, 65, 67, 69, 70-71, 72, 74, 76,
80-81, 83, 84, 87, 88, 89, 90-91, 92, 93, 95, 96, 99, 100, 106-107,
112, 114-115, 116-117, 119, 122-123, 125, 126, 127, 128-129, 131, 132, 137,
139, 140-141, 142, 145, 146, 149, 150-151, 152-153, 154, 157, 168, 171,
175, 177, 178-179, 180-181, 183, 184, 186, 187, 194, 201, 203, 204-
205, 208, 210-211, 213, 217, 219, 222, 244, 225, 227, 233, 234-235,
Back Jacket

Héctor Velasco Facio: 25, 26-27, 28, 35, 40, 41, 42, 44, 49, 52-
53, 54-55, 56, 58, 60-61, 75, 77, 101, 105, 109, 110-111, 121, 161, 163,
164, 169, 170, 193, 195, 196-197, 206, 209, 220-221

Chateau Mouton Rothschild: 167

David Frazier: 102-103

Fotolibra 62-63

iStock 14-15

Justin Concannon: 191

Maison Gerard: 79

Oscar Ruiz C, Imágenes Aéreas de México: 10-11

Shutterstock 134-135, 172-173, 198-199, 214-215

Superstock 22-23, 158-159

Renderings by Alberto Cordoneda: 51, 68

Drawings by Geoffrey Bradfield Inc.: 188-189, 230-231

GEOFFREY BRADFIELD

A 21ST CENTURY PALACE

Mexico City

Architects: López Baz y Calleja

Written by Jorge S. Arango

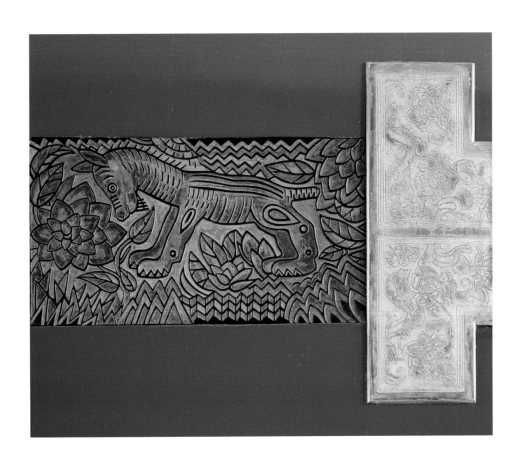

PREFACE

DURING THE RENAISSANCE, it took but 15 years for architect Bartolomeo to build the Palazzo Medici in Florence for Cosimo de' Medici. A relatively brief time frame, perhaps, because the prince kept the exterior restrained, rejecting a more ostentatious design by Brunelleschi. And, as he feared, Giorgio Vasari later wrote, that it would "arouse envy among the citizens."

But in essence, de' Medici did the same thing that all great palace builders do: harness the most incandescent talents of the age—architects, artists and artisans—to conjure a residence of such exquisiteness that it came to symbolize the apex of human achievement in 15th-century Florence. Frescoes by Benozzo Gozzoli, statues and bas reliefs by Donatello, and an altarpiece from Filippo Lippi's workshop, amongst other treasures. Visiting in 1459, Galeazzo Maria Sforza was so awed that he described it as a "*cassoni* of inestimable workmanship and value." Palace-building, in other words, has always been about connoisseurship.

The connoisseurs of our own time are modern-day Medici whose wealth and aesthetic discrimination make possible the building of a new generation of palaces. Thanks to new technologies and advanced machinery, these rare and exceptional edifices rise from the ground with astonishing velocity. Nowadays, their lavishness is more often refracted through the prism of modernity, a "less is more" ethos manifested not in gilded detail, but in precious materials and unforgiving craftsmanship. And they are no longer necessarily walled residences surrounded by expansive parks and hunting grounds. Globalization has stimulated a wholesale rethinking of the palace concept. *TIME* magazine called globalization "an epoch, as surely as the Bronze Age or the Industrial Age," adding that "it is happening with unprecedented speed and scope." Against that backdrop, today's palaces might just as frequently take the form of sprawling high-rise penthouses surrounded by a moat of security: the gatekeeper is the concierge, surveillance cameras are the new palace sentries.

Yet for the palace builders of the 21st century themselves, little has changed. To claim that title, they must still embody that rare talent: the ability to recognize unparalleled artistry and excellence, often before it is acknowledged by the reigning arbiters of taste or validated by history and, through their patronage, to propel art and architecture forward into the next great epoch.

In our contemporary times, an elite coterie of palace builders commission Geoffrey Bradfield. He is known, not without reason, as "the Billionaire's Designer." After more than 40 years creating exceptional residences for many fabled families of the world, Bradfield today is working at the height of his powers. He is a designer who takes risks—because risk, he says, "is, for me, part of the creative vocabulary of being alive." And risk, albeit taken with an assured hand, is what his clients desire.

His work has become more and more reductive over the years, its sense of luxury exquisitely distilled. And his is, unapologetically, a "signature" style. "Design that has come to represent eras—Classical, neo-Classical, all the *Louis*, Gothic, Art Nouveau, Art Deco, High Tech and so on," he says, "are all the result of designers with distinct signatures." Just as surely as de' Medici sought Bartolomeo's particular touch to his palazzo, the tycoons, royals and princes of 21st-century industry seek out Bradfield's stamp of impeccability and daring.

"There is no magic formula for challenging the present," says the designer. "What counts is the know-how, the passion and the will to stay in the fray and remain relevant."

This book introduces the 21st Century Palace series. Each book will take readers on a tour through a particular project, examining its materials, architecture, art collections and antiques, and illustrating the concatenation of ideas and elements that coalesced to create a modern-day palace.

*Palace-building has always been
about connoisseurship.*

*"Quality is never an accident;
it is always the result of high
intention, sincere effort,
intelligent direction and skillful
execution; it represents the wise
choice of many alternatives."*

—WILLIAM FOSTER

Geoffrey Bradfield and his associate, Roric Tobin, 2011.

INTRODUCTION

THERE IS NO GREATER PLEASURE for a designer than clients with whom he shares a profound symbiosis. It is *divine grace* when that relationship of collaboration and mutual respect arcs over many years, resulting in not one, but a multitude, of remarkable, diverse projects. Designer and client mature together, each venture challenges what they know and compels them to push against new boundaries to realize something unlike anything that preceded it.

The clients for this palatial residence overlooking Chapultepec Park in Mexico City were just such a couple. Bradfield first started working with them when their eldest child was just eight years old. That was over 30 years ago, and the family is much expanded since then. Bradfield has attended their birthday parties, their weddings and their christenings. "We have grown up together in many ways," he says with obvious affection.

The clients were both born into privilege. The husband is a remarkably accomplished man, a prince of industry. His wife is beautiful and elegant. They are the quintessence of modern Medici—accustomed to wealth, influential and secure in their identities. In fact, there is something positively regal about them. Bradfield has shepherded over a dozen matchless projects for them: city and country residences, corporate offices, a jet, a yacht.

PREVIOUS PAGES: Aerial view of Chapultepec Park.

When they are in Mexico City, they preside over an ethereal cloud kingdom like those in Japanese *ukiyo-e* paintings, sequestered high above the quotidian world and surrounded by beauty. It is a modern, state-of-the-art palace that levitates over a legendary palatial residence of another time (and, notably, the only royal castle on the American continent). Its long and illustrious history began in 1725. Most famously it indulged the glittering court of the ill-fated Emperor Maximillian and his consort, Empress Carlota.

Today Chapultepec Park boasts nine museums, another synchronicity it shares with his clients' apartment. This floating sanctuary houses a magnificent collection of historic arts of its own—painting, sculpture and priceless furnishings from every quadrant of the globe. Over their years together, Bradfield has witnessed his clients' tastes grow more and more refined. This residence reflects an exquisite echo of their possessions, which mine a plethora of cultures and epochs and represents each one's pinnacle of artistic achievement. Bradfield combined these with a luxuriously minimalist sensibility that gets to the absolute essence of art. This is a story about being able and worldly enough to know 'where and what' is the very best.

Globalization has stimulated a wholesale rethinking of the palace concept.

Winter Palace, St. Petersburg

A SENSE OF PERSPECTIVE

The Entrance Foyer

SERGEI DIAGHILEV'S OFT-UTTERED DECLARATION, "Astonish me!" describes not only what he expected from others, but what he demanded of himself. He was an unrepentant sensualist devoted to beauty so ravishing that it took one's breath away. In a letter Jean-Pierre Nouvel wrote to the composer Igor Stravinsky after the death, in 1929, of this brilliant light behind the Ballets Russe, Nouvel described Diaghilev as "a Dionysian pagan," adding, "He died in love and beauty, under the tender smile of those gods whom all his life he passionately served and worshipped."

There is little doubt that the clients and designer on this project nurture a comparable devotion to beauty. One need look no further than the dazzling collection of art the clients have amassed over more than three decades to see how singular their pursuit of beauty has been. The challenge they shared with the architectural team of Alfonso López Baz, Javier Calleja and Eduardo Hernandez was to create a setting for that collection—and for the family's equally dazzling lifestyle—that would truly astonish.

Visitors emerge from steel-gated private elevators into a barrel-vaulted space, where they are immediately confronted by what the art dealer Paul Kasmin has described as the "graphic purity" of Robert Indiana's *Love* sculpture. This icon of 20th-century Pop Art sets the perfect mood. Originally conceived in 1964, the artist's ambitions for this concept were not unlike the team's own desired intention. "I always wanted bigger and bolder *Loves*," Indiana told *The New York Times* in 2003. Of course, grand proportions were already an inherent fact of this undertaking. It was architectural boldness that they strove to supply.

RIGHT: Robert Indiana was famous for employing the graphic vernacular of American road signs, apparent in his iconic work of Pop Art, *Love*, a herald to the central hall that follows.

NEXT PAGES: From the barrel-vaulted entrance foyer the scene includes work by, from left to right, Yoshitomo Nara; a *Pomme de Ben* sculpture by the Lalannes; one of Donald Judd's characteristically rigorous box constructions; and a painting by Oaxacan-born modernist Rufino Tamayo.

Pitti Palace, Florence

A FORUM FOR ART

The Central Hall

THOUGH THE BARREL VAULT IS HARDLY MODEST, it is nevertheless more discreetly proportioned in order to create a transition from the lower-slung space of the entrance foyer into the vaster rooms beyond. It is a concept pioneered by the legendary Frank Lloyd Wright, who termed this idea "compression and release," and it had been used in medieval places of worship throughout Europe, Central and South America for centuries. The intent was to create a feeling of awe when moving from introductory vestibules of these buildings into the towering volumes of Gothic cathedrals.

That is precisely the feeling elicited here when passing from the entrance foyer to the central hall. The effect is an exhilaration, like being swept up in a sudden zephyr. The ceilings immediately soar exultantly to 30 feet. The space is monumental, and the drama the architects achieved within it is nothing short of spectacular. They had to contend with all manner of structural challenges. But where they could not remove a beam, it was incorporated into the whole symphony of materials and composition.

PREVIOUS PAGES: The central hall, with its majestic scale, functions both as a contemporary courtyard connecting spaces and floors, and as an exhibition environment for great works of international art—two turquoise lacquer doors by Jean Dunand, ancient imperial Foo dogs from the Chiat Gallery, a totemic bronze sculpture by Rufino Tamayo and a Roy Lichtenstein oil.

LEFT: Frank Lloyd Wright's principal of "compression and release" is evident as one enters the hall. Wright believed that moving into a room of exultant heights after a low-ceilinged space physically simulated the American experience of freedom, an appropriate sentiment for a room that freely mixes eras, cultures and artistic genres.

PREVIOUS PAGES: A Roy Lichtenstein work depicts the Ernie Bushmiller comic-strip character Nancy, caught in a blizzard.

THESE PAGES: Bradfield positioning the Lichtenstein work. A detail of the artist's signature pixilation (right).

A pair of 17th-century Qing Dynasty imperial Foo dogs from Chait (the
second concealed by a support column), the earliest objects in the gallery-like
space, possess the resonance of ages. They stand guard, much as they would
at a palace or temple, on either side of the entry.

PREVIOUS AND THESE PAGES: Purchased from Benjamin Steinitz, the lacquer doors were conceived by Jean Dunand in conjunction with fellow sculptor Jean Lambert-Rucki in the 1920s. Part of a set of six pairs, their provenance is impeccable, having been used in the office of Jean Bloch, decorated by Ruhlmann. By showcasing them in this way Bradfield "captured their real value as art pieces" observes Steinitz.

A cantilevered bronze staircase with leather treads projects from a monolith of Portoro marble, framed against a wall of white gold leaf. Beneath the stairs, the surreal apparition of Lalanne's *Pomme de Ben* sculpture. On the second floor, a comely Fernando Botero nude in white marble and more paintings by Tamayo.

The central hall is a symphony of intersecting planes in different luxurious materials. The apple image appeared early in Claude Lalanne's work but took on an oversized scale starting in 2005. Here, one of these *Pomme de Ben* sculptures sports a crouching monkey on its stem, created by her husband, François-Xavier.

Entering the central hall, one is confronted by the coveted works of Rufino Tamayo, Donald Judd, Yoshitomo Nara and François-Xavier and Claude Lalanne—instantly establishing the idea that one has entered a royal repository of international, diverse and peerless art. Within this context, this hall also functions as a palace courtyard, that cloistered inner sanctum where the private lives of aristocrats could unfold away from the eyes of mere mortals.

The walls of this "courtyard" are clad in immaculate white limestone save for one, which owes its otherworldly luminosity to the white gold leaf that sheathes its entire height and breadth. Dominating the center of the hall is an enormous slab of black and gold Portoro marble off which the architects cantilevered, almost impossibly it seems, a bronze staircase with aged dark cognac leather treads. The handrail is a simple ascending channel that has been hollowed out of the Portoro. The floors are a golden marble, a wavy grain book-matched throughout, creating an almost molten sense of flow.

A view across the "courtyard" gives a sense of the processional length of the space, which culminates in a dramatic portrait by Alex Katz.

This portrait by Alex Katz is a
later work by a mature artist who has
evolved from flat, graphic imagery to
surprisingly subtle usage of dimension
and shadow. The dark bronze Tamayo
totem abstracts a familiar motif from
his paintings: the sliced watermelon.

The art one has already encountered is but a tantalizing glimpse of the wonders that populate this space. Inhabiting it are exceptional paintings and sculptures by contemporary masters Fernando Botero, Alex Katz, Roy Lichtenstein, and more Tamayos, as well as porcelain imperial Foo dogs from 17th-century China made during the reign of Kangxi, the fourth Emperor of the Qing dynasty, and a rapturous pair of turquoise lacquer doors designed by Jean Dunand and fellow sculptor Jean Lambert-Rucki circa 1927.

The Dunand doors were purchased from B. Steinitz in Paris, and they are of such rich caliber and flawless craftsmanship that they transcend their function. Bradfield hung them as art, slightly raised from the wall and illuminated from behind. In fact, it has always been his philosophy that fine antiques should be treated as sculptural objects in interiors. "Geoffrey has a way of naturally reacting to quality that does not take into consideration the particular period from which an antique comes," says Benjamin Steinitz. "His combinations are really exciting and creative. It's completely modern without being a clash."

The breathtaking verticality of the space, the sense of procession, the visual and conceptual narrative amongst the works on display, the preciousness of materials and the pitch-perfect lighting all conspire to create a visual ballet that would astonish anyone ... including the exacting Diaghilev.

Massive intersecting volumes create a sense of monumentality and provide dramatic ways to experience the art, which is viewed around corners or glimpsed through stairs and archways.

LEFT: A detail of the Rufino Tamayo painting embodies the artist's particular blend of Mexican folkloric imagery with influences of European modern primitivism and Cubism.

NEXT PAGES: The work, its grand scale rare for Tamayo, injects a splash of brilliant color on the white gold-leaf wall. Tamayo, considered a national treasure, is celebrated with a museum devoted to his art in Chapultepec Park.

ABOVE: Bradfield's rendering of the central hall as envisioned.

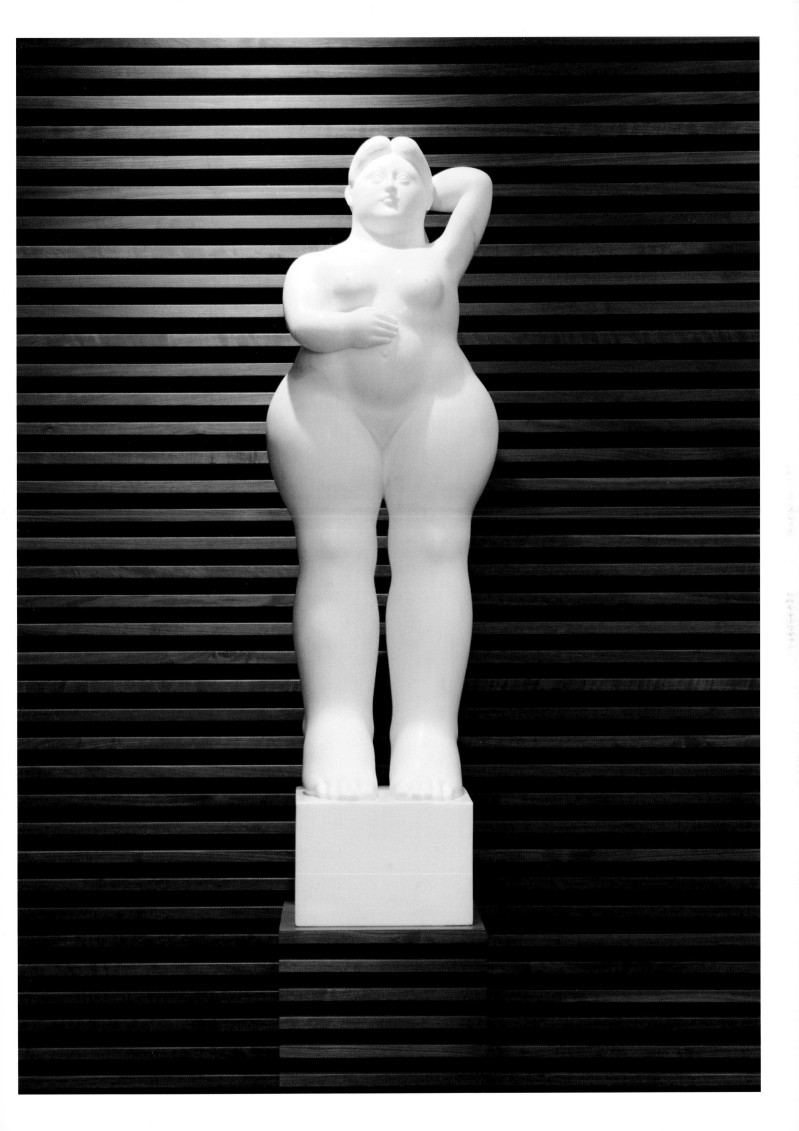

*"Architecture should speak
of its time and place, but
yearn for timelessness."*

—FRANK GEHRY

PREVIOUS PAGES AND LEFT: The view from the second floor landing
makes plain the extraordinary attention to the layering of materials and geome-
tries present in the central hall. A mezzanine lounge is an elegant sky pad from
which to enjoy open-plan views surrounded by the abundance of art.

NEXT PAGES: Another view of the second floor landing with a painting of
watermelon by Tamayo on the left, and a sun-spectacled portrait by Alex Katz
on the right.

Buckingham Palace, London

A FEMININE MYSTIQUE

The Living Room

AFTER ONE OF HIS FREQUENT VISITS TO SUNNYLANDS, the 200-acre winter estate of Walter and Leonore Annenberg in Rancho Mirage, California, President Ronald Reagan wrote in the guest book: "You've made it hard for us to go back to the universe." Designed by A. Quincy Jones in the 1960s and decorated by William Haines and Ted Graber, Sunnylands was a modern Xanadu. The coursing, razor-straight lines and monolithic lava walls of the austere edifice startled the rugged desert terrain to life. It housed, arguably, the most renowned collection of French Impressionist art in the world.

It was this mythic residence that served as muse for Bradfield during the two days required to place and hang a king's ransom of art. Even after a lifetime devoted to the pursuit of art and beauty, Bradfield experiences the handling of works of this caliber, amassed over decades by his discerning clients, as an enormous privilege. His clients looked on as the designer thoughtfully positioned priceless paintings and sculptures about the apartment. The committed trio were acutely aware of the evolving dialogue respiring amongst the various works.

Andy Warhol's powerful sextet of one of his most enduring subjects, Jacqueline Kennedy Onassis, hangs in the entrance to the living room; on the Macassar ebony table, a Degas bronze bather. Occupying center stage, Aristide Maillol's bronze voluptuary draws one's eye to Nature's panorama beyond.

In the living room over a sofa, Bradfield hung a Toulouse Lautrec, flanked on the right by a 1932 representational Picasso portrait of his lover Marie-Thérèse Walter and, on the left, a Matisse gouache. As he stood back scrutinizing the grouping, Bradfield sensed something amiss and soon defined it as the Matisse. While unquestionably ravishing, it exuded an entirely different aura than the Picasso and the Lautrec. It might seem presumptuous to quibble about a work of art of this quality, but as any truly visionary designer will tell you, his first responsibility is to his own creativity. So, only partially in jest, Bradfield turned to his client and said, "You know, the Matisse, although a stunner, is not quite perfect in this grouping. Perhaps you should look for a companion Picasso to complement the romance of the Marie-Thérèse."

ABOVE: Bradfield's rendering of the living room as envisioned.

RIGHT: A personification of grace, a detail of the Maillol.

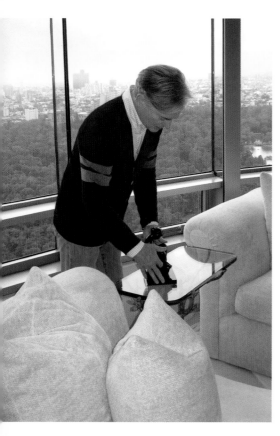

The husband digested the suggestion and, after a moment, rose to the challenge. "Yes, let's look for one together," he agreed. They then continued on their way through the apartment with purpose, situating the remaining works. Three months later, the designer received a call from his client's office. A Picasso portrait of Marie-Thérèse had surfaced at Gagosian Gallery on Madison Avenue, which the client was considering. Would Bradfield kindly avail himself, view the painting and offer his opinion? Today, the Gagosian purchase, an alluring modern abstraction of Marie-Thérèse also dated 1932, is a perfect counterpoint to the one Bradfield's client already owned. Pure alchemy—these miracles made possible by the magic wand of taste and wealth!

As surprising as his client's explicit trust in Bradfield's artistic instincts may seem, another signature aspect of the designer's work has always been the way he inspires clients to create unparalleled collections of art and fine objects. Parisian art dealer Jean-Gabriel Mitterand believes Bradfield cultivates in these clients "a passion for art." With this client, however, the passion was shared from inception. "It's all about our ongoing search for the visually sublime," says Bradfield.

Bradfield in the act, cautiously handling one of Degas's rare bronze bathers. Degas used the medium of sculpture privately to explore dynamics of movement and muscular tension. They were never intended for public exhibition (especially after the chilly reception he received at the sixth Impressionist exhibition in Paris in 1881 for his famous mixed-media sculpture *The Little Fourteen-Year-Old Dancer*, where critics accused him of brutishness). Most were made of clay, wax or plasticine and were not cast in bronze until after his death in 1917, when his heirs authorized a series of editions to be made from 72 of the more than 150 sculptures found in his studio.

LEFT: Warhol was captivated by current events. This image of Jackie Kennedy, part of a series he returned to repeatedly, derives from wire-service photos of the first lady awaiting the casket of her husband, John F. Kennedy. Some, pointed out the art historian David Lubin, have likened it to Benjamin West's neo-classical depiction of Agrippina—the stoic wife of the slain Roman general Germanicus—saying it portrays "a morally significant historical occasion with emotional restraint, muted tones, and architectonic control." But other academics claim Warhol was commenting on the media, citing the artist's explanation that, "What bothered me was the way television and radio were programming every-body to feel so bad."

ABOVE: Upon entry to the right is an exceptionally rare cabinet by Jules Leleu in rosewood with ebony and mother-of-pearl inlay. "It is a major, major work," says Gerard Widdershoven of Maison Gerard, where the cabinet was purchased. "A similar piece, with slightly different dimensions, is in the Mobilier National, France's National Furniture Repository." Above it is a still life by Frida Khalo.

Two views of the Leleu cabinet, which also features bronze sabots and detailing. The vignette includes one of Rembrandt Bugatti's more Cubist-influenced panther sculptures. "Bugatti created an incredible body of work during his tragically short lifetime," says Nick Kilner at Sebastian+Barquet gallery in New York. "Yet it is his depictions of big cats that are most sought after by collectors and remain, for many, his most important and captivating works." An intriguing visual tension has been created by Bradfield uniting the extraordinary refinement of the Leleu with the organic form of the Bugatti and the primitivist imagery of the Kahlo still life.

"The Art Deco period epitomized the neoclassical wave that crashed upon French culture in the years after World War I."

–HERBERT MUSCHAMP

The living room's assembly of masterpieces is a premier example. It is the first impact one has of the stunning setting that surrounds this floating palace. From the spectacle of the central hall, visitors have already caught an enticing slice of the glorious urban view beyond an Aristide Maillol bronze nude. The entrance to the room is paved with a collar of the same Portoro marble as the wall from which the bronze-and-leather entry stair is cantilevered. It serves as a contemplative "pause" between entirely different emotional and aesthetic galaxies—from the obsidian blackness of the Portoro monolith and the soaring heights of the central hall, to the explosion of light and horizontality one experiences in the living room. Cross this threshold onto the polished limestone floor and you can feel your spirit swell infinitely over the landscape.

Fanning outward from a phalanx of floor-to-ceiling glass, Chapultepec Park is one of the greatest urban greenspaces in the world (and the largest in Latin America). It is partially bisected by the stately Paseo de la Reforma and bordered by some of the most eminent residential and commercial districts in this metropolis of millions. In the distance is the majestic volcano-capped Sierra Madre Oriental. "We deliberately took a modern approach to the fenestration," says Bradfield, explaining that there are no traditional curtains here that might obscure or detract from the vistas. Privacy was never a concern, since the space is sequestered so high above, and far away from, the fray. But when the flaming brightness of a Mexican afternoon threatens to overwhelm, the touch of a button activates shades that roll down from pockets in the ceiling.

PREVIOUS PAGES: The art and furnishings in the living room create a soothing sense of symmetry, one made even more serene by the profusion of subtle fabrics and rich materials. On the wall are, from left, an abstracted 1932 Picasso portrait of his lover Marie-Thérèse Walter, a Toulouse-Lautrec and another 1932 Marie-Thérèse portrait by Picasso. Two Henry Moore sculptures are at left; a bronze Fernando Botero dove and a silver abstraction of a female form by Alexander Archipenko are at right.

Toulouse-Lautrec's famous fin-de-siècle paintings and prints of nightlife at
the Moulin Rouge in Montmartre, where he lived and worked, are evidence
both of his livelihood and his downfall. An aristocrat drawn to the
demimonde of Paris, and in particular to the decadence of absinthe and
scarlet women that suffused it, the artist's career spanned a mere 20 years.
Unreconciled to his deformities (he was just four-and-a-half feet tall), he
sought solace in loose living, and died of debauchery in 1901 at age 36. Like
many of his paintings, this portrayal of the famous nightclub's sinful delights
is unquestionably sensual. But it also emits a certain melancholy imparted
by an artist attracted to its darker consequences.

Unlike Lee Annenberg, with her 1960s penchant for color, Bradfield reined in the living room palette, restraining it to a sensuous array of taupes, ivories and creams. "The voice of the room had to be the art," he insists, "so decoration is pared to a minimum." Minimum, that is, enriched by startling subtlety, for the textures are resolutely luxurious. There are three individuated seating areas, the main grouping at its center. It is here that we find the perfect syzygy of the Marie-Thérèse portraits elegantly bracketing the Lautrec. Gazing around the room from this vantage point, one gradually perceives that another Muse was clearly directing Bradfield's hand: Venus, the Roman goddess of love and beauty. The art in this room is a palpable celebration of femininity.

As this Circean reality dawns, the idea that one of Maillol's voluptuous sirens has been the one to usher visitors into this space suddenly begins to make delicious sense. "I express myself in sculpture because I am not a poet," the Catalan-born Maillol once said. But Maillol was, in truth, a most eloquent visual poet of the female form. And in one of those wondrous cosmic coincidences, there is yet another exquisite congruity looming in the air here: A year before the building of Sunnylands, André Malraux, France's Minister of Culture, a man as enthralled with modernity as the Annenbergs, determined that Maillol was the greatest sculptor of his age. He collaborated with the artist's last model, Dina Vierny, to replace all the neoclassical statues in the Place du Carrousel—the famous palais gardens of the Tuileries in Paris—with an irresistible seraglio of Maillols.

When critics declaimed Picasso's portrait of Gertrude Stein, saying that she did not look like that, his riposte was nonplussed: "She will," he said, tersely summing up the hegemony of the artist's vision over mere human perception. Clearly Picasso saw his subjects through a singular lens, as evidenced by this 1932 portrait of his lover Marie-Thérèse Walter. It is unlikely that she ever came to resemble this visage; but Picasso's use of color and line was not meant to be taken literally. Rather, it conveys something deeper about her eroticism. The feminine wiles are continued in two shapely Henry Moore abstractions of the female form (at left and on the coffee table).

Other artists similarly enamored of this subject matter are also represented in this seating area. There are, of course, the two Marie-Thérèse portraits adjoining Lautrec's wanton sybarites living it up at the Moulin Rouge. An abstract Henry Moore sculpture placed to the side of the central sofa is unmistakably feminine, as is a more recognizable reclining Moore on the low table and a curvaceous polished-silver Alexander Archipenko sculpture opposite. A sated Fernando Botero dove invokes Greek mythology, where the bird was classically associated with Aphrodite.

Two matching custom sofas and a pair of bespoke armchairs complete this seating arrangement and surround two massive bronze low tables with surfaces swathed in luxurious stingray crisscrossed by brass inlay. The entire assemblage sits atop a rug designed by Bradfield. "I wanted it to have a feeling of liquid in motion," he explains, "to look as though a pond had just been gently disturbed by a breeze." The resulting silk and wool creation veritably ripples underfoot.

Another Picasso portrait of Marie-Thérèse Walter represents her in more figurative terms, though in similar colors. Unlike other mistresses, who Picasso portrayed in dark and brooding shades, Marie-Thérèse was always awash in pastels and bright tones. Picasso began his affair with her when she was just 17. When she became pregnant with their daughter Maya, Picasso's wife, the Russian dancer Olga Khokhlova, left Paris for the south of France with their son Paulo, though they never divorced. Also painted in 1932, this image hints at Marie-Thérèse's alluring youth (she was just 22, while Picasso was 51). Picasso eventually took up with Dora Maar. To the right is a silver abstracted female figure by the Kiev-born Cubist sculptor Alexander Archipenko. Accessories contribute to the sense of luxury. The silver box, part of the clients' collection of silver objects from Bulgari, is typical of the company's harmonization of classical and contemporary, displaying an ancient coin set into a modern silver form. Nicola Bulgari, says Benny Tabatabai in VIP client development, is an avid collector of Greco-Roman and Persian coins, and pieces highlighting them "are some of his favorites because they harken back to his forebears, who were silversmiths before they were jewelers."

Diana Widmaier Picasso, granddaughter of the artist and Marie-Thérèse, told Tina Brown's *The Daily Beast* in April 2011 that, at first, Picasso disfigured Marie-Thérèse to hide her identity from his wife. But she believes that, in addition, the 1930s, "was a very experimental period," for Picasso. "He was hiding her from himself. He was telling his own story."

Widmaier Picasso calls the affair between her grandparents, "one of the great love stories in art history." This idyllic representation attests to the artist's tenderness toward her youth and beauty. The scholar John Richardson has called Marie-Thérèse "the one woman in Picasso's life who was really his soul mate."

PREVIOUS PAGES: Like the panorama, this view of the living room creates a procession of vistas from foreground to background, mirroring the sprawling splendor of the city outside.

LEFT: This furniture grouping, which includes a Diego Giacometti branch table and cat sculpture, affords an inviting view into the dining room beyond, with its Lalanne statue.

RIGHT: During the installation, Tobin and the client's majordomo position chairs commissioned by Bradfield.

To one side of this central conversation area is the Maillol, which presides over two comfortably upholstered armchairs and a Macassar ebony Ruhlmann table inlaid with ivory (on the table, a Degas bronze). Against the wall here is a masterpiece of Art Deco by Jules Leleu, a stunning cabinet purchased from Maison Gerard in New York. Its body is rosewood, a gorgeously figured material in its own right. But it also showcases an intricate floral inlay of ebony and mother-of-pearl designed and executed by Méssager, the French lacquer and marquetry master who frequently collaborated with Leleu.

"It took over 3,000 hours of handwork to accomplish," marvels Maison Gerard's proprietor Gerard Widdershoven. In the context of all this womanly presence, the inlay could be a metaphor for a lush Garden of Eden. Upon it skulks one of Rembrandt Bugatti's sinewy bronze panthers. And above, a Frida Kahlo still life proffers, like Eve, a tempting array of exotic forbidden fruit.

Bradfield acquired this double-tiered Macassar ebony table by Ruhlmann. Reviewing the Ruhlmann exhibition at the Metropolitan Museum in 2004, Herbert Muschamp wrote: "Ruhlmann practiced an art of making wood look wealthy. No pine need apply. Instead, we move in the exclusive company of amarynth, amboyna, palissander, rosewood and kingwood. The wood veneers are burnished to such a high degree of polish that they almost pass for rare minerals."

At the other end of the room a quartet of Deco-inspired chairs commissioned by Bradfield encircles another Macassar ebony Ruhlmann table with ivory inlay. A cabinet as stupendous as the Leleu was needed to balance the room, so for this grouping Bradfield turned to eminent 20th-century decorative arts dealer Anthony DeLorenzo on Madison Avenue in New York. DeLorenzo's solution was an extraordinary rectangular pedestal chest, also by Ruhlmann. Made of American burl walnut, it bears an octagonal bronze plaque by S. Foucault depicting a bare-breasted nymph. "It is one of only two we've owned in the past 30 years, and is one of our favorite pieces," explains the gallery's director Adriana Friedman.

"We've been dealing with Geoffrey Bradfield since the 1980s," notes DeLorenzo. "He was one of the very first designers to see the importance of Ruhlmann and recognize the other leading de-signers of the French Art Deco period. At a time when there were only a few 20th-century decorative arts collectors, Geoffrey had the foresight to see the importance of this market and encouraged his clients to acquire these works of art."

Hanging above it and completing the female theme is a peerless Frida Kahlo self-portrait. "There are very few Kahlos in private hands," marvels Bradfield, again admiring the exceptional refine-ment of the collection.

Spend time in this room and one might feel the same brand of melancholy experienced by President and Mrs. Reagan at having "to go back to the universe." For what Bradfield has created here, levitating above the verdant parkscape, is a universe of pleasure unto itself.

Above a Ruhlmann cabinet is one of Frida Kahlo's most famous paintings, *Thinking About Death*, from 1943. Though Kahlo did not pass away until 1954, by this point in her life her health was so precarious that she spent many hours each day confined to bed. She was plagued with illness since childhood. At 18 she was in a bus accident that smashed her spinal column and fractured her pelvis. Despite these extraordinarily painful circumstances, she was a prolific artist who championed folkloric imagery and attired herself in traditional Tehuantepec dresses and pre-Colombian jewelry.

"Ruhlmann designed for the class of new rich created by modern industry, families like the Renaults, the Voisins and the Rodiers. He considered them equivalent to the titled aristocracy of the past."

—HERBERT MUSCHAMP

RIGHT: The Ruhlmann cabinet bears a plaque depicting a nymph. "Only a few examples were made featuring different materials and plaque detailing," explains Adriana Friedman, director of DeLorenzo Gallery, where the cabinet was purchased. "This particular example was commissioned in Paris in 1927 by Paul Dormann as a wedding gift for his daughter."

NEXT PAGES: At left, a Yoshitomo Nara painting in the entry hall is visible from the living room. People have interpreted his cartoonish knife-wielding children with their sour expressions as menacing. But Nara has said: "...[the weapons] are so small, like toys. Do you think they could fight with those? I don't think so. Rather, I kind of see the children among other, bigger, bad people all around them, who are holding bigger knives." At right, the juxtaposition of Nara's painting and Kahlo's seems to bear this out. Kahlo was the long-suffering lover of the philandering Diego Rivera. Though she was no innocent herself, she could be seen as an emotional casualty of Diego, one of those bigger, bad people holding bigger knives.

Dining Room, Chapultepec Palace, Mexico City

THROUGH THE LOOKING GLASS

The Dining Room

O NE MORNING ON A VISIT TO PARIS in the early 1990s Geoffrey Bradfield was preparing for a day crowded with appointments when the phone rang in his suite at the Crillon. It was Jean-Gabriel Mitterand, principal gallerist for the husband-and-wife artist duo François-Xavier and Claude Lalanne. Bradfield knew Mitterand well, having collaborated with him over past decades to place the Lalannes' idiosyncratic works in the collections of many of Bradfield's fashionable clients. But he was calling at an uncharacteristically early hour.

"The Lalannes would like to have you over for breakfast," Mitterand informed him. "Can you be ready by eight?"

Bradfield had never met the artists, but he knew enough about them to recognize the rare honor of such an invitation. Quickly rearranging his packed schedule and pulling himself together, he appeared in the lobby at the appointed hour, whereupon Mitterand whisked him off to the home and studios of the legendary artists in Ury, just outside the city. The four sat down to typical country fare—steaming hot chocolate served in immense bowls and oven-fresh croissants—exchanging pleasantries and talking about art, in broken French and English, with the gallant Mitterand acting as interpreter.

The dining room is magical at twilight, when the city's lights are reflected throughout the room by the glass and acrylic surfaces of the furniture, multiplying their glittering effect. Surrounding the Lalanne table, which was custom made to seat 16, are Bradfield's neoclassical Lady Mendl chairs. Beyond, Lalanne's *Olympe II* sculpture.

Bradfield recalls that François-Xavier was quite frail (in fact, an ambulance was idling outside that morning to take him to hospital after breakfast). The couple was modest and unassuming, and typically enigmatic about their art. "It's almost as if they shared a spiritual secret with nature," remembers Bradfield. "Their works were 'in' jokes with our Creator. They weren't going to explain them. You had no choice but to simply experience the joy of them."

At the end of this simple repast, his hosts offered Bradfield a tour of their garden. "They were charmingly competitive," says Bradfield. Claude would point to works and identify them as "his" or "mine." (And indeed, she told *Le Point* in 1974, "We live together and exhibit together. That's all.") "I felt as if I was falling down Alice's rabbit hole," says Bradfield of that unforgettable tour. "The garden had that infantile quality of wonderment, and had the power to completely transport one."

The allusion to Lewis Carroll's most enduring character is often cited and completely natural. The enthusiastically imaginative oeuvre of the Lalannes is as witty, skillfully engineered and hallucinatory as it is utterly unique. Pierre Bergé described it this way: "When desks charge into the clearing of our waking dreams; when knives, forks and spoons collude to form a spiky, flowery parade of silver-gilt; when wool-covered seats begin to bleat...when all these things join in one endless round dance, then I know that you don't have to be Champollion to realize that poetry has arrived."

PREVIOUS PAGES: The name of Alexander Calder's mobile sculpture, *Seven Morsels*, seems an especially apt sobriquet given its placement above the dining room table. It is one of very few Calders made completely in white (the artist favored black and primary colors). Claude Lalanne's *Olympe II* statue was originally made as a fountain for the Sceaux Gardens in Paris. It was modeled after her own grandchild and sports a collar of cast lettuce leaves.

LEFT: To enrich the glamour of the environment and emphasize the Deco inflections of the room, Bradfield designed panels of carved gesso that were then gilded in white gold. They impart the feel of a Lalique cast-glass wall, a clear reference to the décor of classic Deco-era ocean liners like the Île de France and the Normandie. (For the Normandie's first class dining room, which was longer than the Hall of Mirrors at Versailles, Lalique created 12 illuminated pillar torchères and 38 matching columns along the walls.) The screen motifs here—butterflies and flowers—convey the sense of a garden, recalling the fantastical grounds of Claude and François-Xavier Lalanne outside Paris.

It was precisely the Lalannes' magical strand of poetry that served as a springboard for the ethereal design of this dining room perched high above the glittering lights of this Mexican metropolis. And understanding their work is central to understanding the sense of enchantment that looms in the air here like the mists of an incantatory dream.

Bradfield has long recognized the allure of the Lalannes. Years ago, says Mitterand, the designer saw they were "the last living artists of another world, that of sophistication, and one belonging to the recent past—Marie-Hélène de Rothschild, Natalie de Noailles, Yves Saint Laurent—and that their fantastical impression on our imagination is made of surrealistic invention and charm."

For Bradfield, what Gilbert Lascault identified in a 1970 essay for *Paris-Normandie* was always clear: namely that "...these artworks... immediately invoke the world of luxury. A luxury that is not ashamed to declare itself, that rejects discretion and so-called good taste."

From the earliest planning stages of the dining room, Bradfield's design called for a Lalanne sculpture to stand at what he felt was an essential spot, one that would make it visible from the entrance foyer, connecting it thematically to the monkey-topped bronze *Pomme de Ben* at the base of the stair. His renderings specifically stipulated one of the artists' outsized *Lapin Victoire* hares (underlining the *Alice in Wonderland* allusion), "but for some reason, when we began our search, it was impossible to find one with a cabbage collar," he recalls.

PREVIOUS PAGES: Two views of the dining room, where the furniture practically disappears, ceding graciously to the spectacular views. Toward the entrance from the central hall the mass and volume of the furnishings serve as a visual transition from that highly architectonic space into this ethereal one, which seems suspended in midair, floating like a luxuriously appointed zeppelin over one of the largest metropolises in the world.

ABOVE: "They entertain constantly," says Bradfield of his clients. "It's the nature of their culture, which is consummately sociable." Every fête is attended to by their expertly trained staff, which takes great pride in making certain each detail is perfect.

BELOW: The table is ornamented with rare Chinese celadon porcelain from the early 18th century, purchased from Chait Gallery in New York.

Instead, *Olympe II*, a 1984 sculpture by Claude, was located in London. This piece manifests thoroughly the qualities that make *lalannes* (the work so impacted Gallic culture that it spawned a noun to describe it) so captivating. The androgynous figure of an adolescent in a lettuce collar—eyes closed in a reverie that appears to be part dream-sleep, part rapture—lifts a hand skyward as if to tune in to some secret, barely audible celestial music. This beautiful, angelic youth quietly commands a palpable hush that implores visitors to also listen to the delicate, heavenly ether.

The magnificent dining room table is also a Lalanne. Even beyond it's innate beauty and collectability, it is exceptional in two respects. First, for a family accustomed to lavishly entertaining the most elite and powerful personages in the world, it was necessary that the table comfortably accommodate 16 for the clients' epicurean feasts. Bradfield wanted François-Xavier's *Capricorn* table here, but the design had only ever been produced as a smaller version, its glass top held aloft by a single pair of sleek conjoined goats. Lalanne proposed creating a base with double pairs that could support a round glass top with a much greater circumference. This incarnation had never before (nor has since) been produced; it is a completely one-of-a-kind creation. Secondly, and more sadly, it turned out to be François-Xavier's last recorded private commission. "He died in December of 2008 just after we took possession of the table," says Bradfield.

The chairs are upholstered in a mushroom-colored fabric that captures the weave of tapestry or needlepoint, but rendered in a modern idiom.

To enhance the beguiling surrealism with which these *lalannes* infuse the room, Bradfield kept the furniture as transparent as possible, deploying glass and acrylic throughout. Around the table are the barely-there silhouettes of Lady Mendl chairs from his own collection of classically inspired acrylic furniture (exhibited during a 2009 retrospective of Bradfield's furniture at Sebastian+Barquet Gallery in Chelsea). The clear seating and table surface afford unobstructed views of the surrounding landscape and, from blue twilight to yellow dawn, also multiply the sparkling profusion that emanates from city lights and the stars above. The breathtaking sensation is one of being suspended in the midst of an infinitely expanding galaxy.

Overhead glides *Seven Morsels*, a tantalizing mobile sculpture by Alexander Calder. Again, as in the living room, the congruities amongst the various priceless elements of the overall design are startling. Bradfield first saw *Seven Morsels* suspended by itself in a vast industrial warehouse that had been opened on a weekend especially for his client. It was then, and still is, the only completely white Calder mobile Bradfield has ever come across. "It absolutely spoke to one," he recalls. "You knew you were in the presence of something stellar." What Bradfield did not know at the time, how-ever, was that François-Xavier Lalanne was equally transfixed by Calder's work. Lalanne, who throughout his life was consistently inscrutable about the inspirations behind particular pieces, once admitted to an interviewer: "I allowed myself to be seduced by Calder's mobiles. What I liked was the life in them."

PREVIOUS PAGES AND RIGHT: Bradfield, who came to know the Lalannes well over the years, had commissioned several "Capricorn" tables from the couple for clients. But these had featured single figures. Here, these clients needed something larger, so François-Xavier Lalanne proposed a base featuring two figures instead. It is a unique design and the artist's last private commission.

NEXT PAGES: Two sublime cabinets by Ruhlmann, of whom Herbert Muschamp has written: "The edges of his rectangular surfaces are often subtly curved, as if to reproach the obvious. Slender, tapered, the fluted legs tiptoe delicately across the floor like a ballerina en pointe."

Bradfield flanked the entry to the dining room with two panels of his own design that are moulded from gesso and gilded in white gold. The reference is clearly to 1930s French décor, specifically to fabled transatlantic liners such as the *Île de France* and the *Normandie*. "I wanted them to be in keeping with the fantasy world of the Lalannes," explains the designer of the panels, describing their leitmotif as "an ethereal garden of butterflies and flora."

The screens are also a perfect foil for two handsome cabinets adorned with ivory accents by Ruhlmann, a designer intimately entwined, as it happens, with the decoration of the *Normandie*. Purchased at DeLorenzo Gallery, these two substantial pieces stand on slender, tapered legs that give them the appearance—like the rest of the room—of floating in space. Slinking across the top of each cabinet, surveying the whole scene, are two more Rembrandt Bugatti bronze panthers.

To one side is another, smaller glass-topped table, this one by Diego Giacometti. "There is a wonderful correlation between Giacometti and the Lalannes," believes Bradfield. "They had similar fascinations with nature—birds, leaves, frogs and other flora and fauna—but their techniques were totally different. Giacometti's elegance is more primitive in its approach and fabrication; it's like appreciating the raw power of African art. And all three artists loved the contrast between polished and burnished metals and those with matte finishes. The textural juxtapositions make you vividly aware of the materials." Finally, on the limestone wall behind the Giacometti hangs another still life by Tamayo.

The room glimmers undeniably with fantasy and enchantment. But it is most alive with these qualities, of course, during a dinner party, when the air adds voice with intellectual conversation and with confidences exchanged amongst the most formidable empire builders of our time.

PREVIOUS PAGE: "The client has amassed an outstanding collection
of bronzes by Rembrandt Bugatti that includes some of the artist's most
important and iconic works," says Nick Kilner at Sebastian+Barquet gallery.
"Focusing solely on Bugatti's celebrated big cats, his collection spans the
artist's career, charting the course of his stylistic development from the
impressionistic modeling of his earliest renderings to his late, vigorously
modeled and expressionistic sculptures." They sit atop matching Ruhlmann
cabinets from DeLorenzo Gallery.

Diego Giacometti's "... armature and imagery is rustic, yet they also have the majesty of furniture from the medieval and ancient worlds. These objects are functional, yet they retain their identity as sculpture."

—MICHAEL BRENSON
THE NEW YORK TIMES

Rufino Tamayo was orphaned at 12 and raised by an aunt who owned a wholesale fruit business, which explains the ubiquity of colorful fruit in many of his works, particularly still life paintings like the one here. Before it, a table by Diego Giacometti that exhibits his fondness for animal imagery and for mixing metals that were roughly wrought with refined ones, and matte with polished finishes.

Ursino Library, Catania, Sicily

A WEALTH OF MATERIALS

The Library

"A DAY SPENT WITHOUT THE SIGHT OR SOUND of beauty, the contemplation of mystery, or the search for truth or perfection is a poverty-stricken day," wrote the American historian, philosopher and literary critic Lewis Mumford. "And a succession of such days is fatal to human life."

For Bradfield, poverty of any stripe has never been an option. On the contrary, his aim with any room he touches has always been to make it a viscerally rich experience, a place brimming with all the ingredients so eloquently enumerated by Mumford as essential for sustaining life. There are many effective tools he deploys in the service of this pursuit: a rigorously curatorial discretion, a highly developed sensitivity for color and tone, a perspicacious understanding of the harmonies of form.

And then there is texture, the endless experimentation of which has often led to the defining style of many a great artist. Van Gogh had his swirling impastos, Dubuffet his frenziedly scratched surfaces. Pollock had his layers upon layers of drips, Frankenthaler her pooled and diffused stains. "Texture draws the eye of a viewer," wrote the Greek contemporary painter George Politis, "dry-brushing, sponging-on, spattering with paint-loaded brush…Spattered dots become the 'diamonds' that add sparkle even in the darkest shadows." In this library, Bradfield has wielded texture as deftly as these artists wielded palette knife, brush and paint.

RIGHT: "The paintings look easy the way Fred Astaire made dancing look easy and Cole Porter made words and music sound easy," wrote art critic John Russell of Alex Katz, the author of the painting hanging beside the library doors. "But don't let's be fooled. When it comes to the art that conceals art, Katz is right in there with those exemplars." That might explain the sense that, as Leslie Camhi wrote, his paintings are "at once entirely matter-of-fact and oddly elusive."

NEXT PAGES: The success of the library is predicated on exemplary craftsmanship and extravagant materials. Cashmere, suede, gold leaf, crocodile leather, amboyna burl, gilded bronze, Macassar ebony—all these conspire to intoxicate the senses. The persimmon orange and crimson palette refers back to the Katz portrait in the central hall.

The carefully calibrated collage of finishes begins with the supple caress of calfskin leather, which wraps around the bronze handles of the glass doors. Separate the doors and they slide effortlessly into pockets in the wall, leaving one standing upon another interstice of dusky Portoro marble, which marks the transition from the high-gloss gold marble of the entry hall to the warmly organic wood floor of the library. The floor is a subtle mosaic of end-cut oak blocks, an imaginative modern rendition of classic parquet floors so often found in the great chateaux of Europe. Vertically, swathing all but the curtain wall of glass, a soft, pliant invitation of suede is hemmed with a thick band of pale yellow gold-leaf trim.

Dominating the room is a superb Art Deco desk by Ruhlmann purchased at Friedman & Vallois in New York, which injects the handsome figuring of amboyna burl into the textural mix. Alex Barlow, the gallery director, praises this rare, circa 1926 piece for "its purity of line, simplicity of design, and its execution, which is, frankly, a feat of incisive engineering." The massive writing surface seems impossibly balanced on a slender, gently curved cradle. "There's an incredible lightness to it," he observes, "which was a remarkable characteristic of all Ruhlmann's work."

Behind the desk are bespoke Macassar ebony cabinets and étagères meticulously handcrafted by Simon Hamui for the furniture firm of Norma Rodriguez. As one might expect of such an inveterate collector, the shelves display a treasure trove of first-edition books. Another lithe Bugatti bronze panther walks calmly toward the urban jungle outside the windows, seemingly oblivious to a masterpiece of analytic Cubism by Pablo Picasso suspended above. Further down the same console is a gilded bronze box by renowned Italian sculptor Arnaldo Pomodoro. The Bugatti actually completes a sculptural triangle, the other points of which are defined by two additional bronzes: a Henry Moore standing figure framed against the magnificent view and a highly unexpected Cubist piece by Alberto Giacometti on the desktop.

One of Alberto Giacometti's expressionistic bronze heads sits atop a 1960s acid-etched bronze table by Philip and Kelvin LaVerne. The sofa frame picks up the woven leather of the Kyle Bunting rug, which is interspersed with Spanish tile designs rendered in cowhide.

Of course, the journey toward the perfect textural mélange is not simply a matter of taking existing textures and mixing them. It extends to seeking out pieces made by artists and artisans who go to stupendous lengths themselves to create textures that are new or painstakingly specific, people who are innovators within the rarefied microcosm of the materials with which they work. The Hérmès chairs that face the desk exemplify this degree of obsession.

The clients first encountered the chairs on a visit to the famed purveyor of luxury goods. They were captivated by the design, but less enamored with the tan color of the crocodile leather stretched across the seats and backs. So Bradfield requested that Hérmès create another pair using a deeper gray-washed mahogany color of crocodile hide. Hérmès, of course, was happy to oblige and even agreed never to use that same shade on another chair, raising the enterprise to a level of exclusivity that clients like Bradfield's demand. Some time later, one of the chairs arrived. But then several weeks lapsed with no sign of the second chair.

Bradfield's vice president, Roric Tobin, placed a call to Hérmès inquiring about the lone chair's companion. "I'm afraid the crocodile is not *portant* [plump] enough yet," he was told. "You mean you know exactly which crocodile you're using?" asked the bemused Tobin. "Oh, yes," replied the Hérmès representative without apparent irony, proceeding to offer an explanation of the conditions under which Hérmès crocodiles are bred. Raised in Australia, swimming languorously in cashmere-lined glass pools to ensure their hides are never scratched, they must surely be the most pampered creatures in the animal kingdom. Because the finest leather comes from the belly, they are fed lavish repasts for years to swell their abdomens to kingly Henry VIII proportions!

The study in similarities and contrasts around the room creates a stimulating give-and-take. Both the rug and the table are sectioned in squares that appear to mimic tile. But both also alternate disparate textures to dramatic effect (cowhide and woven leather in one case, differently treated bronze in the other).

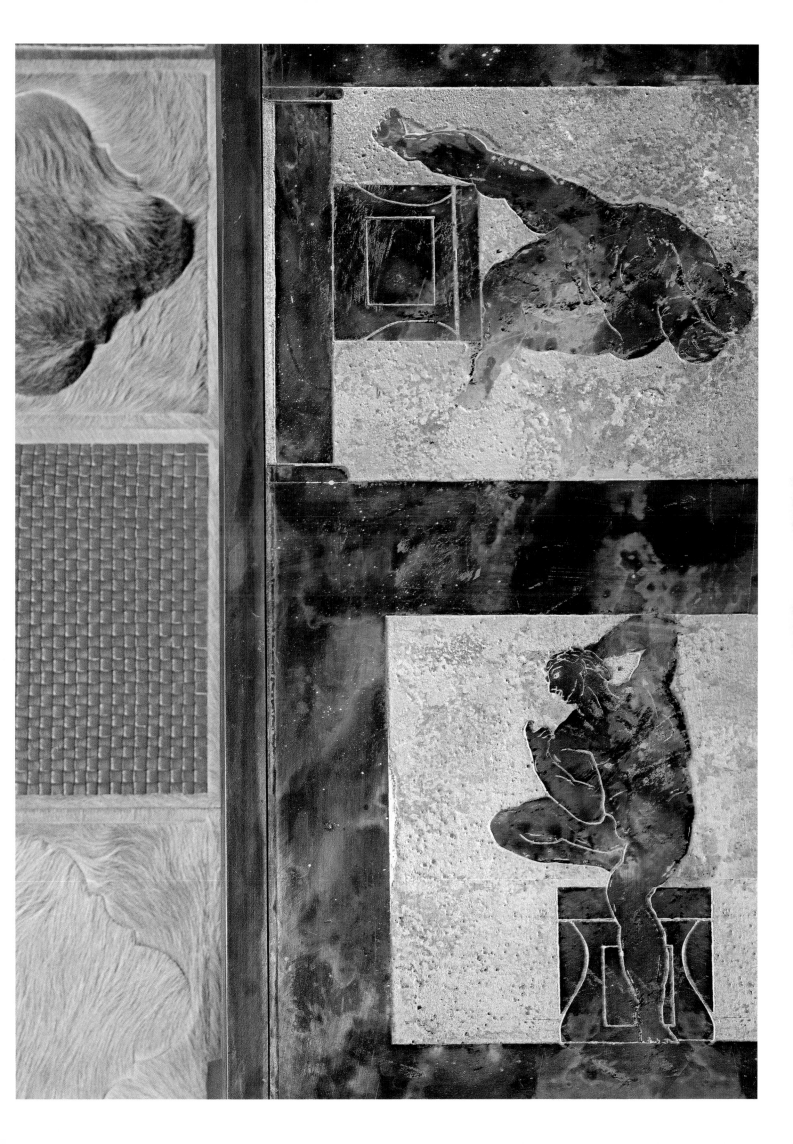

Opposite the desk, the low table at the center of the furniture grouping tells a similar tale about the passion for texture. Discovered by Bradfield at Benrd Goekler in New York, it was made in the 1960s by Philip and Kelvin LaVerne. This father-and-son duo was famous for its historically themed enamel tables, which also featured complexly designed bases. "The engineering doesn't stop at the surface," notes Bradfield admiringly of the asymmetrical arrangement of legs and stretchers holding up the acid-etched bronze slab, which depicts Michelangelo's "Ignudi," the muscular male nudes that support five narrative scenes running the length of the Sistine Chapel ceiling in Rome.

On this particular low table, the LaVernes depicted Michelangelo's "Ignudi," male nudes adorning the four corners of various scenes of the Creation on the ceiling of the Sistine Chapel, the apostolic palace in the Vatican. They caused great controversy because they were not integral to the theme of Creation and seemed, to the pious Popes, a mere excuse for nudity.

The beauty of the LaVernes' work was not only in their flawless craftsmanship however; it was in their innovation. In order to achieve exactly the right patina, the men would bury the furniture in specially treated soil for six weeks. If they were unhappy with the results, they would toss everything and start anew. Placed atop the table is one of Alberto Giacometti's poetically mournful attenuated heads.

Kyle Bunting, who made the rug that grounds this conversation area, is another likeminded innovator. Bunting works almost exclusively with cowhide, which he says people think of as "the redheaded stepchild of leather" despite the fact that "it's tactile, sultry and chic." Bradfield, he says, "is a seasoned aesthete with a reputation for recognizing, early on, things that are transcendent. He came to me and said, 'I have this idea for something that is more mixed media and that integrates woven leather into the design.' It was a great concept and a mechanical challenge," he concedes, "but the result is a stroke of genius." The rug renders the ubiquitous Spanish tile seen throughout Mexican homes in luxurious materials. The woven leather checkers represent, albeit magnificently, terracotta field tiles, and the tone-on-tone cowhide squares stand in for the porcelain-glazed tiles with which they are often interspersed.

RIGHT: Ignudo number nine, from the third bay of the Sistene Chapel. Giorgio Vasari considered these figures the apex of depictions of the body in motion: "...to tell the truth, anyone who is a painter no longer needs to concern himself about seeing innovations and inventions, new ways of painting poses, clothing on figures, and various awe-inspiring details, for Michelangelo gave to this work all the perfection that can be given to such details."

NEXT PAGES: The Ruhlmann desk and the Henry Moore sculpture have the quality of intriguing balancing acts. One can't quite comprehend the engineering that keeps them upright, which adds to their allure.

Bradfield continued the woven leather onto the arms of a custom sofa, which is upholstered in Loro Piana cashmere for good measure. So are the Deco-inspired armchairs to either side of the sofa, for that matter. Finally, a Tamayo painting awash in persimmon and musk-melon oranges, as well as touches of crimson, refers back to the sitter in red, painted by Alex Katz, that arrested visitors at the entrance to the room.

"A designer knows he has achieved perfection not when there is nothing left to add, but when there is nothing left to take away," said Antoine de Saint-Éxupery. And in this sensual assembly of textures—leather, cowhide, amboyna burl, bronze, cashmere, Macassar ebony, yellow gold—who would dare Bradfield to remove a single thing?

PRECEDING PAGES: A vignette atop the console behind the desk expresses a splendid triangulation of objects—a Pablo Picasso painting, a Bugatti bronze panther and a gilded bronze box by Arnaldo Pomodoro—against suede walls.

LEFT: Paolo Volponi's description of Arnaldo Pomodoro's work easily applies to this gilded bronze box: "His three-dimensional surfaces, his spheres and his sections of cylinders have truly been crafted by the workings of time, replete with the forces of history, events, consciousness, fate, will..." But there is also something reminiscent here of his friend Louis Nevelson's assemblages.

The work of Ruhlmann "recalls that the term classical originally denoted class, not mass. It described the language of elites. Seldom can such a tongue have been enunciated more precisely than it is by Ruhlmann."

—HERBERT MUSCHAMP

The complex textural mix—woven leather, tone-on-tone cowhide and end-cut parquet-like oak floors—transforms the library into a highly tactile experience.

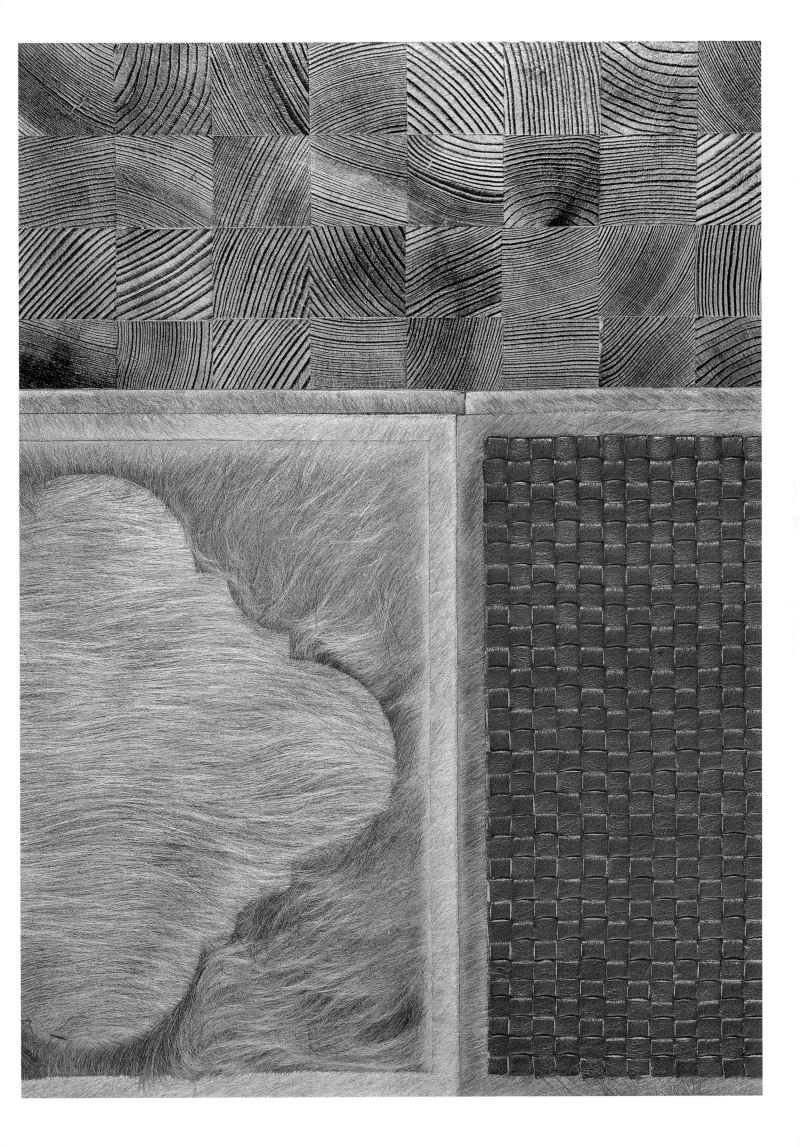

Wine Cellars, Chateau Mouton Rothschild, Bordeaux

AN OENOPHILE'S LAIR

The Wine Room

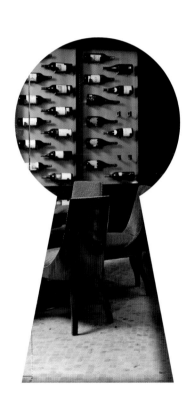

W HEN A FERVENT ART COLLECTOR is suddenly seized by a correspondingly ardent passion for accumulating fine wines, only one collection above all others will slake the thirst of his longing: those rare bottles of Mouton-Rothschild that bear labels commissioned by Baron Philippe de Rothschild from a staggering stable of 20th-century masters.

It is widely recognized that the prestigious program officially commenced in 1945. That year, the baron commissioned Philippe Jullian —the witty illustrator of books by Balzac, Colette, Dostoyevsky, Proust and Wilde—to imagine a design that reflected the sense of jubilation felt by the French people over the return to peacetime after the psychological and emotional devastations of World War II. Jullian's concretion of the Dionysian ideal took its cue from Winston Churchill's famous victory gesture: the iconic two-fingered "V" sign.

Since 1945, a veritable Who's Who of painting and sculpture's glitterati have relished the opportunity to contribute to this celebrated campaign: Cocteau ('47), Braque ('55), Dalí ('58), Miró ('69), Chagall ('70), Kandinsky ('71), Picasso ('73), Warhol ('75), Keith Haring ('88), Francis Bacon ('90), Antoni Tàpies ('95), Lucien Freud (2006). The recompense consisted of two cases of wine, one from their label year and the other from a different vintage. Of course, there is something also to be said for rewards reaped by aligning one's ingenious talents with perhaps the most famous name in viticulture. The artists have only one restriction: that their artwork relate to one, or a combination, of three themes—wine, the pleasure of imbibing it, or the ram (the symbol of Château Mouton-Rothschild).

The wine room's modern décor is intended as a counterpoint to the more traditional Spanish-style wine cellar designed for the clients' ranch. It also reflects its more sophisticated urban setting and features high-tech LED lighting and modern engineered materials. The table is surrounded by fine Art Deco chairs acquired from Sebastian+Barquet.

After Baron Philippe's death in 1988, his only daughter, Baroness Philippine, assumed control of the selection and commissioning of artists. She continues today, broadening this elite creative club to mirror the multicultural nature of contemporary art. Her globalized, forward-thinking view has had a surprising and immediate impact on the collectability of bottles in the series. After her announcement that Nanjing-born artist Xu Lei would produce an ink painting for the 2008 label, trading of that Mouton-Rothschild vintage skyrocketed by 20 percent overnight and began selling for a breathtaking £10,000 per case.

Bradfield had the honor of meeting the baroness in 2007 in New York. She had curated a traveling exhibition of original paintings created for the labels that was timed to coincide with an auction of wines from her private cellar at Sotheby's. It was during a private gala for Mouton-Rothshild's top collectors (who eventually opened their pockets to the tune of over $2 million that storied night), that the designer conducted a lively conversation with Baroness Philippine. "She exuded that very French aura of alluring confidence. Gowned in burgundy silk and sporting *big jewelry*, she reminded me of the ageless actress Simone Signoret," recalls the designer. "She was extremely gracious."

The choicest bottles from rare and extraordinary vintages take pride of place on vertical racks behind the tasting table. Varying the method of display adds visual variety to what could have been a monotony of row upon row of shelves.

Of course, an example of each of these bottles lies aging here in the wine vault of this palatial residence. The client's collection even includes the hard-to-come-by Balthus nude nymphet that in 1993 so scandalized the United States Bureau of Alcohol, Tobacco and Firearms that its sale was banned there. He also owns the chaste, white-labeled version that sold in its place on American wine boutique shelves. Naturally, Bradfield's client is a man of many worldly tastes and also happens to be a discerning oenophile. So his Mouton collection keeps fine company with priceless bottles of Châteaux Petrus, La Tâche and Yquem, with Dom Perignons and Cristals.

Bradfield describes the stylish design for the space as "very Ian Fleming,"—cool, clean lines and theatrical lighting. It was intentionally created as a counterpoint to the more ornate Spanish colonial wine cellar designed for the clients' country ranch, which featured wrought iron wine storage, stone floors and vaulted ceilings. And indeed, one could easily see 007, post shaken (not stirred) martini, suavely plumbing the pleasures of a Châteaux Margaux '66 here.

Hundreds of wines line up uniformly along the walls, comfortably recumbent on notched modern shelves handcrafted by Simon Hamui for the furniture firm of Norma Rodriguez. They are encased in thick plate glass, which emanates a high-tech blue glow as light from the LEDs above the vitrines disburses through them. A display wall highlights the most rare and precious elixirs, including jeroboams of Petrus. A circular glass-topped tasting table illuminated from within permits one to gaze on other treasures while seated on elegant Art Deco chairs.

The original germination of Rothschild's concept for artists' labels dates to the 1920s. At the time Baron Nathaniel (Philippe's grandfather) purchased this chateau in the Médoc, vintners sold their production by the cask to a merchant who then aged, bottled and marketed the wine. In 1924, Rothschild took the revolutionary step of performing these delicate processes within the hilly confines of the hectares that had produced it, and then branded and marketed the wines himself. To commemorate this historic departure, he commissioned the most famous poster artist in France, Jean Carlu, to create a label that in turn made history of another kind: it signaled the first time the influence of Cubism appeared in the graphic arts.

1945
ANNÉE DE LA VICTOIRE

TOUTE LA RÉCOLTE MISE EN BOUTEILLES AU CHÂTEAU

1945
Cette récolte a produit
24 jéroboams numérotés de A à Y.
1475 magnums numér de M1 à M1475
74422 bouts½ bout. numér de 1 à 74422
2000 Réserve du Château marquées R.C.
Cette bouteille porte le Nᵒ R.C.

Philippe de Rothschild

Château
Mouton Rothschild
APPELLATION PAUILLAC CONTRÔLÉE

SPÉCIMEN

de J. Cocteau

TOUTE LA RÉCOLTE MISE EN BOUTEILLES AU CHÂTEAU

1947
Cette récolte a produit
26 jéroboams numérotés de A à Z.
20 double-magnums numér. de DM1 à DM.20
2170 magnums numér. de M1 à M.2170
57558 bout.&½ bout. numérotés de 1 à 57558
4000 Réserve du Château marquées R.C.
Cette bouteille porte le Nᵒ

Philippe de Rothschild

Château
Mouton Rothschild
APPELLATION PAUILLAC CONTRÔLÉE

SPÉCIMEN

Dessin inédit   de Henry Moore

1964   1964
Cette récolte a produit :
167.444 Bordelaises et ½ Bᵗᵉˢ de 1 à 167.444
2.580 Magnums de M1 à M. 2.580
87 Grands Formats de GF1 à GF87
double-magnums, jéroboams, impériales
3000 Réserve du Château marquées R.C.
Cⁱᵉ R.C.

Philippe de Rothschild

Château
Mouton Rothschild
BARON PHILIPPE DE ROTHSCHILD PROPRIÉTAIRE A PAUILLAC
APPELLATION PAUILLAC CONTRÔLÉE
TOUTE LA RÉCOLTE MISE EN BOUTEILLES AU CHÂTEAU

SPÉCIMEN

Gouache inédite de Kandinsky _ Mouton Rothschild 1971

1971   1971
Cette récolte a produit :
224.386 Bordelaises et ½ Bᵗᵉˢ de 1 à 224.386
1750 Magnums de M1 à M. 1750
180 Grands Formats de GF1 à GF180
double-magnums, jéroboams, impériales
5.000 Réserve du Château marquées R.C.
Cⁱᵉ.

Philippe de Rothschild

Château
Mouton Rothschild
BARON PHILIPPE DE ROTHSCHILD PROPRIÉTAIRE A PAUILLAC
APPELLATION PAUILLAC CONTRÔLÉE
PRODUCE OF FRANCE
TOUTE LA RÉCOLTE MISE EN BOUTEILLES AU CHÂTEAU

SPÉCIMEN

JOHN HUSTON

In celebration of my beloved friend
Baron Philippe's 60ᵗʰ harvest at Mouton
John Huston

Château
Mouton Rothschild
1982
ma 60ᵉᵐᵉ vendange Baron Philippe
tout en bouteille au Château
APPELLATION PAUILLAC CONTROLEE
Baron Philippe de Rothschild g f a
PRODUCE OF FRANCE   PROPRIÉTAIRE

75 cl

SPÉCIMEN

Dessin inédit de   K. Haring

1988
toute la récolte a été mise
en bouteilles au Château
Philippine de Rothschild

Château
Mouton Rothschild
12.5% Vol.   PAUILLAC   75 cl
APPELLATION PAUILLAC CONTROLEE
Baron Philippe de Rothschild g f a
PRODUCE OF FRANCE   PROPRIÉTAIRE

SPÉCIMEN

1853 - 2003
Adjudication
en faveur de Mr le baron
nathaniel de Rothschild
du Domaine Brans Mouton
...

2003

SPÉCIMEN

Dessin inédit de   Lucian Freud

2006
toute la récolte a été mise
en bouteilles au Château
Philippine de Rothschild

Château
Mouton Rothschild
13% Vol.   PAUILLAC   75 cl
APPELLATION PAUILLAC CONTROLEE
Baronne Philippine de Rothschild g f a
PRODUCE OF FRANCE   PROPRIÉTAIRE
ALC. 13% BY VOL. - RED BORDEAUX WINE - PRODUCE OF FRANCE - 750 ML.

SPÉCIMEN

Dessin inédit de   Xu Lei

2008
toute la récolte a été mise
en bouteilles au Château
Philippine de Rothschild

Château
Mouton Rothschild
13% Vol.   PAUILLAC   75 cl
APPELLATION PAUILLAC CONTROLEE
Baronne Philippine de Rothschild g f a
PRODUCE OF FRANCE   PROPRIÉTAIRE
ALC. 13% BY VOL. - RED BORDEAUX WINE - PRODUCE OF FRANCE - 750 ML.

SPÉCIMEN

ABOVE: Bradfield and Tobin being offered one of their client's priceless bottles of Chateau Petrus.

RIGHT: An entire case of wine can be accommodated beneath the glass table surface, which is illuminated from within, creating a theatrical and innovative form of display worthy of a classic 007 film.

It was on these chairs that Bradfield and his vice president, Roric Tobin sat with their clients in the apartment after it had been installed. To commemorate the occasion, the client determined that the first bottle of wine to be opened, naturally, would be stellar. His majordomo was instructed to decant a luscious bottle of burgundy—a Châteaux La Tâche Domaine de la Romanée-Conti '78, deemed by wine experts to be one of the top 100 bottles to try before one departs this life.

"One could easily become accustomed to this," says a satisfied Bradfield. "I can eliminate that from my list of life's pleasures and aspirations."

LEFT: The handsome wood grain of the vertical display is a fittingly luxurious backdrop for bottles from some of the best-known wine houses of Bordeaux.

ABOVE: The client's majordomo reviewing the inventory of Petrus jeroboams.

Royal Bed Chamber, Versailles

LUXURIOUS ZEN

The Master Bedroom

IT IS NOT HYPERBOLE TO CHARACTERIZE the bedchambers of mid-17th-century Bourbon monarchs as only fleetingly concerned with privacy and refuge. During what is universally recognized as one of the longest and most illustrious reigns in European history, the cosseted life of Louis XIV and his family was on almost round-the-clock public display. Against this supremely privileged tableau in the era preceding the French Republic, it was perhaps inescapable that Louis should revive the Medieval practice of holding court in his private apartments.

A nobleman at Versailles could aspire to no more exalted an honor than an invitation to the *Lever du Roi*, the ruler's awakening ritual. The centrality of the state bed in the political affairs of these *ancien régimes* dictated that they more closely resembled thrones than places of relaxation and repose. The silk brocade fabrics were of such Byzantine complexity that they could be hand-loomed only at the painstaking rate of just three centimeters a day.

This grand tradition largely disappeared after the French Revolution. In the wake of the storming of the Bastille, European royalty felt it prudent to adopt a less immoderate comportment as a strategy for preserving, unlike the ill-fated Louis XVI and his consort Marie-Antoinette, their powder-wigged and bejeweled crowned heads.

Rising out of Chapultepec Park is the former palace of Emperor Maximilian and his consort, Carlota. The *doré* legs of a 1960s table are a subtle modern reminder of the gilded pleasures of that storied court.

*"After one has played a vast
quantity of notes and more notes,
it is simplicity that emerges as the
crowning reward of art."*

—FREDERIC CHOPIN

PREVIOUS PAGES: A continuous bamboo forest
rendered in a progression of luxurious materials sweeps upward,
beginning with the highly sculpted pile of the wool-and-silk
rug, moving to the silk damask of the custom bed clothes and
culminating in a breathtaking white-and-honey onyx wall.

RIGHT: A detail of the 1960s *doré* table beside the window.

Contemporary sovereigns are far more guarded about their private lives, preferring their bedrooms to embody sanctuaries to which they can escape from the pressures of their imperial duties. It is precisely this aim that this sumptuous master suite was determined to achieve. However, in Bradfield's eyes, modern discretion has never implied an equivalent diminishment of luxury. The discipline of materials showcased here reflects the same level of thoughtfulness and creative genius that Charles LeBrun brought to the decoration of Versailles.

The panoramic view unfolding outside the windows is Chapultepec Park's lush carpet of green. The stately presence of Emperor Maximilian and Carlota's castle rises out of the trees, a reminder of another, more opulent, age. Bradfield's response was to contrast this class of grandeur with a more restrained modern splendor that manifests in extravagant, impeccably edited materials and furnishings.

"What was absolutely key here was to achieve a sense of serenity," explains Bradfield, who cast his eyes to the East—specifically that archetypal symbol of serenity, the Zen garden—for inspiration. Bamboo became the dominant motif, rendered here in three luxurious iterations. Thanks to the miracle of today's technology, the crafting of materials proceeds at a swifter pace than three centimeters per day. Nevertheless, the silk carpet's sculpted pile, in a soothing palette of mushroom and cream, still took eight months to complete. "Geoffrey wanted us to match the onyx wall exactly, right down to the stems of each bamboo stalk," says Joseph Britt at Stark Carpet, which executed the design. "We had to send a graphic designer down to Mexico to create a specific template. He definitely challenges you to exceed what's expected."

LEFT: A Ruhlmann cabinet minimally adorned with ivory accents is a sculptural presence against a wall in the master bedroom. Its streamlined classicism is perfect in a room dedicated to a modern sense of luxury. Ruhlmann was reacting against, Herbert Muschamp writes, "19th-century Romanticism and everything it stood for: preening emotion, heroic bombast, loss of control."

NEXT PAGES: Bamboo motifs take on different characters when rendered in varied materials: wool and silk (left) and two tones of onyx (right).

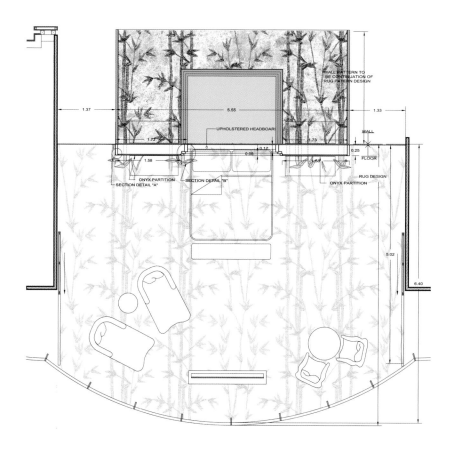

The bamboo motif continues onto the bedclothes, here depicted in hand-quilted damask silk from Scalamandré. Finally, a headboard of supple suede is set into what can only be described as an acme of the stonemason's art: a custom-designed twenty-by-ten-foot wall of backlit white and honey-colored onyx portraying an abundant bamboo forest. The monolithic design required almost 1,200 pounds of stone to execute. Bradfield's vice president, Roric Tobin, traveled to Carrara to select the stone used here. "We didn't want the whitest of white onyx," he explains, "because there is no movement in it."

And, indeed, the bamboo stalks of this spectacular wall do seem to sway as if in a calming forest breeze. The two varieties of onyx—the whiter background and the honey-toned vegetation—are of equal thickness, pieced together like a jigsaw puzzle into a single inspired composition. The stone carvers who created this masterpiece, recalls Tobin, were simultaneously hard at work on pilasters and other ornamentation destined for the palace of Vladimir Putin. Incredibly, Bradfield and Tobin prevailed upon these artisans to accelerate production of the onyx bamboo glade, forcing the Russian prime minister to take an unwitting backseat.

Grandly proportioned bedside tables of Bradfield's design, wrapped in champagne-hued exotic wood veneer and topped by rock crystal lamps and Maillol bronzes, complete the vignette.

Aside the window, overlooking Chapultepec Park, is a seating area. The *doré* branch legs of a 1960s table rise from the floor to grip a three-inch-thick disc of clear acrylic. "It resembles the setting for an exquisite diamond," observes Bradfield, "almost like signature Buccellati." Two bespoke armchairs upholstered in carved silk velvet make it an ideal place to take one's morning tea. Off to one side is another fine Ruhlmann cabinet of amboyna burl with ivory accents.

LEFT: The floor plan for the master bedroom reveals the complete luxury of uncluttered space in the master suite.

BELOW: A diagram delineating the dimensions and concept for the spectacular onyx wall into which the suede headboard is set.

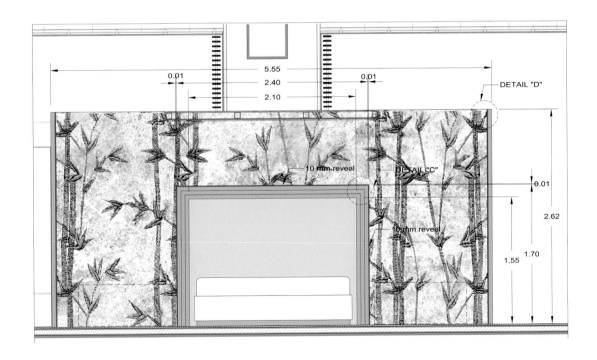

*"The sculptor's hand
can only break the spell to
free the forms slumbering
in the stone."*

—MICHELANGELO

The master baths were to express a level of personal indulgence nonpareil in the world today. Again, Tobin is our dragoman in Carrara: "We drove up winding mountain roads in a tiny Fiat, occasionally having to swerve precariously to yield to the trucks traveling back down from the quarries laden with tons of marble; there is no way they could have stopped!"

Tobin selected only the choicest slabs, those that exhibited the most desirable veining and translucence. The client had been very taken by a hand basin he had seen in a luxury hotel suite and he had asked Bradfield to replicate a similar design for his bath. A large block of rock crystal was selected and hauled to the workshop where, Tobin recalls, "diamond blades ran round the clock for three weeks" to hollow out a sink. For the wife's bath, the team claimed dramatically figured marble that was fastidiously book-matched to cover huge expanses of walls and floor. The color of that figuring ranges from pale gray to fawn in order to complement the bleached wood and stainless steel drawers of the vanity and cabinetry.

Roric Tobin at the stone yards in Carrara, Italy, where he hand-selected the onyx that would be used for the master bedroom's bamboo wall, a segment of which is behind him.

Perhaps more than anywhere else in this residence, the sublime minimalism and monochromatic palette of the master suite exemplifies the qualities promulgated by the great classic modernists: purity of form, dignity of materials and simplicity of line. The confluence of these culminates in a level of elegance not reliant on the sort of ostentation that led the residents of Versailles to the guillotine. Excess is avarice, after all. Elegance, on the other hand, is an attitude. And as the Dutch computer genius Edsger Dijkstra observed, elegance "is not a dispensable luxury, but a factor that decides between success and failure." By that calculus, this environment succeeds beyond all possible measure.

His master bath is a composition of intersecting horizontal and vertical marble planes. The material was selected for its exquisite luminosity and dramatic veining. In the foreground is a crocodile leather stool from Hérmès.

THESE PAGES: By day, the sink, which required three weeks of round-the-clock cutting to hollow, enjoys a backdrop of majestic volcanoes in the distance. By night, the mirror's reflection appears to be a window into another world.

NEXT PAGES: Her master bath becomes a showcase for the stunning veining of the marble. The vanity looks out over the sprawling urban splendor of the capital.

Hall of Mirrors, Versailles

COUTURE COMFORT

The Guest Apartments

THE PREVAILING MYTH OF VERSAILLES is that it was the epicenter of 17th-century fashion and luxury. Of course, this is partially true, and movies like Sofia Coppola's cinematic bonbon "Marie Antoinette" do nothing to dispel the legend. The aura of Louis XIV's court certainly exuded an irresistible gravitational pull. "While most courtiers had comfortable homes near the royal palaces," writes the historian Eleanor Herman, "they coveted the honor of lodging under the king's roof." But being fashionable, as we know, can be a double-edged sword.

In the wake of the War of the Fronde—when nobility attempted to weaken the Sun King's powers and the populace essentially held the royals hostage in their own palace—Louis served his vassals a humiliating comeuppance: he made proximity to his majesty a rank of status while simultaneously ensuring that proximity would be fairly disagreeable. As a 1958 review of a book about life at Versailles put it, "...the highest families in France were crammed with appalling discomfort into icy garrets."

So there is little doubt that those abject souls would have greeted the guestrooms and baths of this residence with gratitude. The rooms, intended as they are to house children and grandchildren, are relatively simple and unburdened by a need to impress. But while it was unnecessary that they approach the level of lavishness of other spaces, Bradfield's and his clients' own design standards demanded a certain sense of couture. And these are, unquestionably, couture environments, where materials and palettes caress and flatter the inhabitants.

Everything is custom. The designers sheathed both guestroom floors in hand-woven leather, which provides a pampering cushion for one's step. The weave is designed to simulate wood grain, an ingenious sleight of hand made all the more elegant by virtue of the fact that it is not readily apparent; it is another layer of luxurious detail that one notices only after spending time in the room.

The barrel-vaulted second-floor elevator foyer brings together a Baccarat floor lamp by Philippe Starck and Jenny Holzer, and a limited-edition bench imbedded with 288 LED lights, originally conceived in 2008, by the German industrial designer and light objects artist Ingo Maurer.

Atop these are bespoke wool and silk rugs that take their cue from the custom bedcovers, the rug patterns enlarging and abstracting those patterns to, at once, create contrast and continuity. The fabrics are a soft blend of chenille and silk, linen and velvet. Bed throws are ultrasuede. Even the millwork's linear planes, which appear to be suspended above the floor, have a lightness of being. "There is an essential sense of economy," says Bradfield, "but they really are luxe."

Powder rooms and bathrooms spare no expense either. Every vanity is custom. The marble of floors and surfaces is hand selected to complement wood grains and amplify light. In the library powder room, the vanity and walls are entirely swathed in semi-precious tiger's eye—a gemstone believed to bring about wellbeing that also attracts wealth and good luck.

And of course, there is outstanding art, particularly an Alex Katz tree painting in one of the guestrooms. "Rather than observing a scene from afar, the viewer feels enveloped by nearby nature," Katz said of this series of paintings, which he used to explore variations on the way light fell through branches. "I wanted an environmental landscape, where you were *in* it."

The same can be said for these spaces, which make it possible to experience couture from a more intimate vantage point than the fashion runway or the pages of a magazine. In these rooms, one is actually *in* it.

PREVIOUS PAGES: This guest room is like a well-tailored ensemble, its custom rug design smartly coordinated, like a pant or skirt to a jacket, with the pillow fabric—Bergamo "Optik 13"—on the bed. Above the beds is a relatively tame charcoal drawing by Hector Javier Ramirez, a Guadalajara-born artist known for his surreal themes. Believing that "animals are more human than the humans," his work is often about the Sublime (in the Romantic sense of the term).

LEFT: A guest bath's vanity is framed in beautifully figured walnut and has an organic, handmade quality that is nonetheless completely modern.

ABOVE: Another guestroom with views of Mexico City. The floor here
is leather woven to imitate wood. Atop it is a sculpted wool and silk rug.
The painting is by Alex Katz.

RIGHT: A guest bathroom's vanity takes a traditional form and reinterprets
it through a sleek, modern lens, mixing bleached wood, stainless steel and
marble. The apartment is so high and away from the bustle of the city that
privacy is not an issue.

*"Luxury must be
comfortable, otherwise
it is not luxury."*

—COCO CHANEL

PREVIOUS PAGES: After a large retrospective at the Whitney Museum of American Art in 1986, Alex Katz began concentrating on landscapes, specifically on the subject of light as it fell through trees. Here this subject is explored in an urban setting, the light coming from the moon and the apartment building behind the trees.

RIGHT: In a private sitting room for the guest apartments, a work by Fernand Léger and another by Tamayo keep company with a Lalique Tourbillon vase. The Tourbillon vase was originally designed by René Lalique in 1927 in clear and black glass and depicted the turbulent currents of wind. It has since been reproduced, in limited editions of 999 pieces, in Cap Ferrat blue, citrine yellow and opaque black.

Topkapi Palace, Istanbul

A MATTER OF CUSTOM

The Game Room

FEW FAMILIES CAN BOAST the prolific artistic pedigree of the Milanese Bugattis. Carlo Bugatti (1856-1940) was an eminent designer of jewelry and furniture during the especially fecund period of Art Nouveau. His eldest son, Ettore (1881-1947), who became a naturalized French citizen, founded the eponymous car manufactory in Molsheim, Alsace, that turned out such outstandingly crafted automobiles that they were collected like great works of art. Another son, the aptly named Rembrandt Bugatti (1884-1916), was a sculptor whose muscular depictions of wildlife continue to be covetously sought after at the world's top auction houses and galleries.

Ettore, in fact, did not identify himself merely as a car designer. Rather, he considered himself first an artist who applied the same concentrated scrutiny and perfectionism to his oeuvre that DaVinci or Rubens did to theirs. His legendary high-performance vehicles—so sleekly ravishing that they became emblems of the Art Deco period through ubiquitous depictions in the graphic arts of France—were glorifications of the finest craftsmanship. Hand-scraped engine blocks were so flawlessly level that they required no gaskets. Valve covers, dashboards and many of the engine compartments' exposed surfaces were intricately engraved with guilloché patterns, a technique that jeweler Carl Fabergé paired with enamel to adorn precious Easter eggs and other gifts he created for the tsars of Russia.

Bugatti automobiles were such singularly magnificent machines that they sometimes drove bankers, nobles and playboys across the European continent to irrational passions. It could reasonably be said that the dashing gigolo Louis Chiron's obsession with Bugatti automobiles was what impelled him to serially seduce wealthy women at the dance halls of Monaco and Nice. And, of course, it was her unconquerable longing to ride in a Bugatti (paired with the lithesome youth of the driver) that led to Isadora Duncan's tragic death.

A Rufino Tamayo work hangs near one of several models of antique Bugatti cars. Ettore Bugatti produced stunning feats of automotive engineering that were works of art in themselves. They came to represent the forward momentum of modernity during the period of Art Deco.

So it is not mere happenstance that Bradfield's client is an intensely fervent connoisseur of masterful workmanship. He is the owner of a fleet of Ettore's cars, as well as Ferraris, Maseratis and other antique and contemporary automobiles (in addition to a spectacular customized G550 Gulfstream jet). An avid racer himself, he is zealous about the precision required to build anything truly exceptional.

This drive for the ultimate in everything extends to all aspects of his life. Even the fact that casual comfort and relaxation were the primary aims of the game room in this Mexico City residence could never justify the slightest slackening of this standard. The room is, like Ettore Bugatti's racecars, a glorification of fine craftsmanship, as well as a distillation of luxury.

The room is enfolded in fastidiously executed millwork that handsomely mixes ebonized and driftwood tones. A cube-like volume in one corner appears accented with the thin elongated gray bricks so loved by modernists such as Neutra and Schindler. Closer inspection reveals, however, that these "bricks" have actually been deftly swaddled in costly shagreen, the stingray skins hand-selected to mimic the various color gradations that characterized that omnipresent midcentury material.

One side of this well-appointed architectural volume opens to reveal a bar. Next to the bar is a table that looks like a crosscut section of a petrified tree trunk. Unlike an ancient sequoia, of course, the archly named "Gepetto" top did not take hundreds of years to make. But the design, created by Kate McIntyre and Brad Huntzinger for their Berkeley, California-based atelier, Ironies, is still the product of a labor-intensive process. It sits on an "Aslo" base of hand-forged iron, surrounded by custom chairs that are sheathed in sensual orange and beige leathers.

PREVIOUS PAGES: The overall view of the game room clearly confirms its emphasis on meticulous craftsmanship. A lively cinnabar orange punctuates the driftwood gray millwork and furnishings in a room designed to be a comfortable gathering place for family. The shelves are filled with models of custom cars commissioned by the client—an avid racer—for his vast auto collection.

LEFT: What appear at first to be thin gray bricks are actually blocks wrapped in precious shagreen, which adds another layer of sensual tactile sensation in an already richly textural space.

Occupying the rest of the space is a seating area where the family gathers for recreation and to engage in the activities of a rich and loving domestic life. Yet even here, each element was required to exhibit remarkable craftsmanship. "Geoffrey is creative and very demanding," says Joseph Britt at Stark Carpet, which has produced Bradfield's rug designs for 30 years. "We make a lot of exacting samples, varying the height of the pile, adapting color with every grouping and regrouping of fabrics."

Here, the carpet is deceptively simple—taupe and orange stripes. But hours were spent calculating how thick and thin to make the pile to ensure both durability and comfort within the context of this more rambunctiously treated room. "It's about grandchildren," says Bradfield, implying, modestly, that the room's aspirations are somehow more prosaic. Yet, sit in this environment and one will feel enveloped in supple, caressing textures and understated surfaces that at first glance may not reveal the exacting processes involved in their making.

And if one should peruse the display shelves, he or she will find a collection of models representing the client's yachts and jets, as well as antique model cars, the latter of which comprise, of course, many of his inimitable Bugattis.

LEFT: A door in the wood and shagreen "cube" opens to reveal a bar stocked with Lalique and Riedel crystal. A table is surrounded by chairs upholstered in beige and Hèrmes orange leather.

ABOVE AND NEXT PAGE: The stone top of the table, commissioned from Ironies through Jerry Pair, was cast using custom colors and resembles the crosscut trunk of a petrified tree.

*"Nothing is too beautiful,
nothing is too expensive."*

—ETTORE BUGATTI

As creative forces continue to rethink and redefine a deco-
rating vision for this new century, Geoffrey Bradfield and his
associate, Roric Tobin, find themselves constantly airborne
. . . introducing their unique brand to current projects as far
reaching as Shanghai, Jakarta, Tokyo, Jerusalem and Dubai.

The astonishing advance of technology, making Design
positively global.

ACKNOWLEDGEMENTS

This book could never have been realized without the trust and cooperation of my generous clients. To these wonderful patrons, I extend my most heart-felt gratitude.

I wish to give special thanks to my associate, Roric Tobin, whose collaboration and contribution to this project have been invaluable to me. I must also acknowledge the creative efforts and talent of my in-house graphic designer, Justyna Watorek. Not least, my close friend Helena Lehane for her keen critique and encouragement.

A special thank you to my publisher, John Smallwood, and his designer Tara Romeo, at Smallwood & Stewart, for their professionalism and shared vision.

Also indispensable to the production of this book was my writer, Jorge S. Arango, a man of infinite patience and gifted perception.

I would like to express my pleasure in our collaboration on this project with the inspiring team of architects, Alfonso López Baz, Javier Calleja, and Eduardo Hernandez, and millwork designer, Simon Hamui. It is a boon to work with professionals of this caliber.

Thank you to the exceptional photographers: Sean Finnigan and Héctor Velasco Facio.

I have always been in awe of Julian Schnabel and am indebted to him for his generous insight.

Lastly, my thanks and admiration to the gallery owners and antique dealers who have lent authority to the chapters: Tony De-Lorenzo; Adriana Friedman at DeLorenzo; Benny Tabatabai at Bulgari; Nick Kilner at Sebastian+Barquet; Gerard Widdershoven at Maison Gerard; Alex Barlow at Friedman Vallois; Benjamin Steinitz; Jean-Gabriel Mitterand; Steven Chait.

I continue to be enriched by their knowledge and expertise.

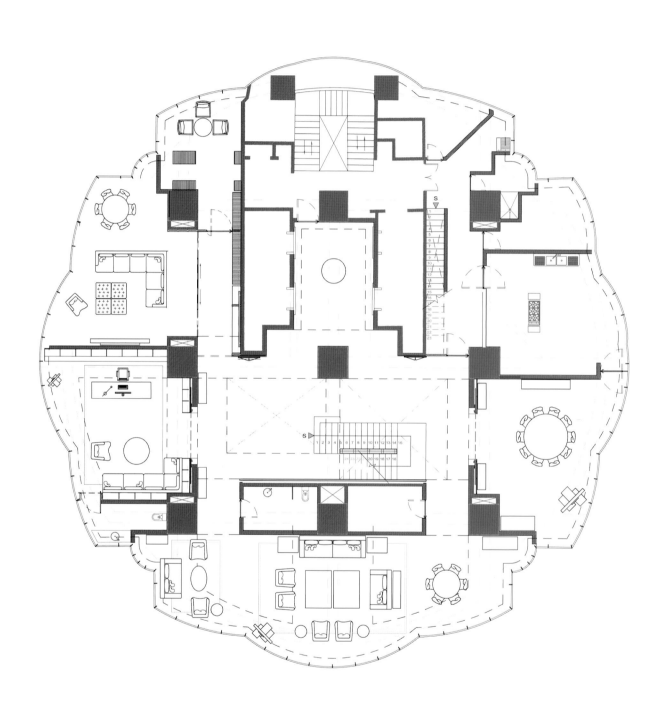

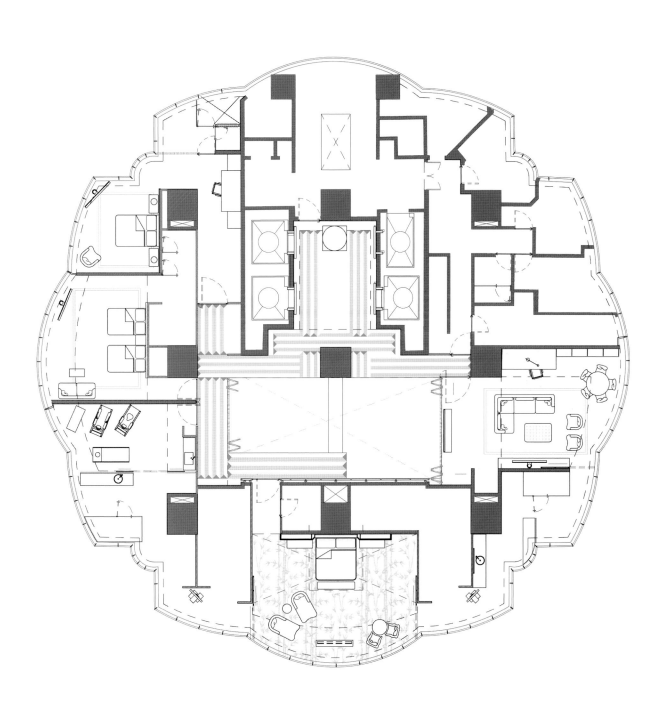

"Life is short, art endures."

—HIPPOCRATES, 'APHORISMS'

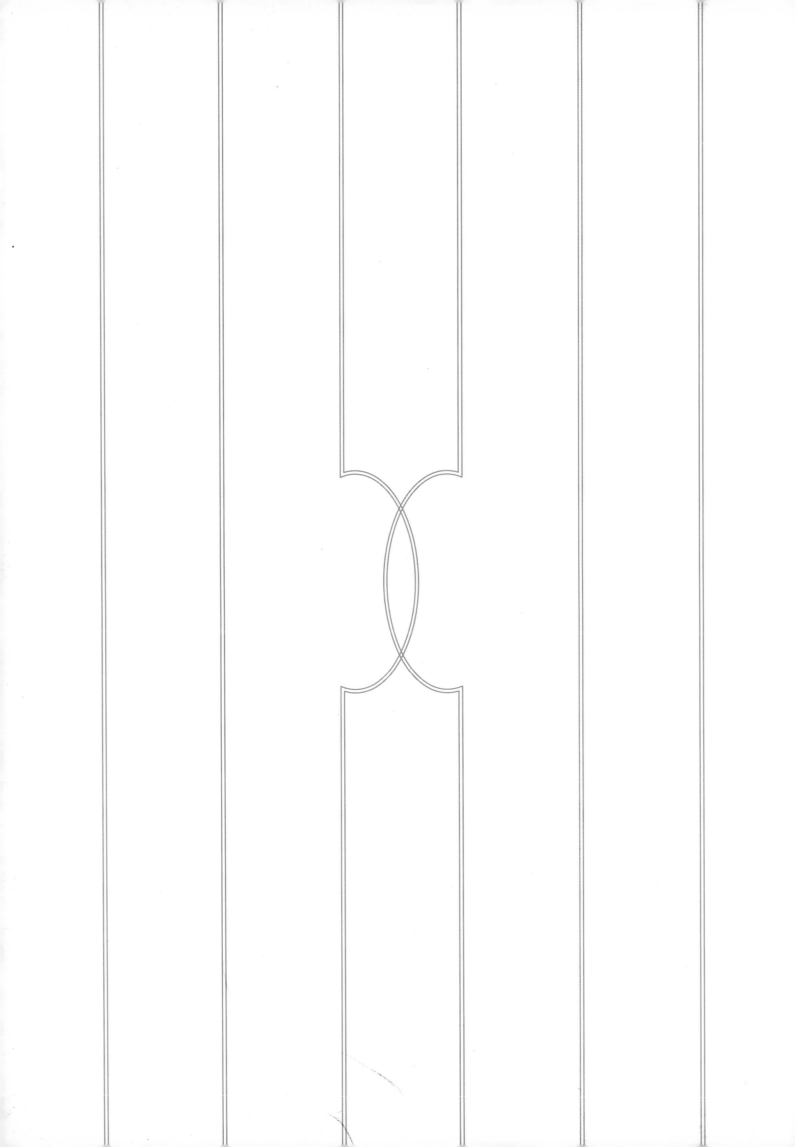